Royal Commission
on Local Government
in Scotland

WRITTEN EVIDENCE

12

Stirling and Clackmannan Joint Police Board
Dumfries and Galloway Police Committee
Association of Scottish Police Superintendents
Scottish Police Federation, Joint Central Committee
Central Fire Area Joint Committee
Chief Fire Officers' Association
Fire Brigades Union
Association of Civil Defence Officers, Scottish Region
Local Government Auditors' (Scotland) Association
Institute of Chartered Accountants of Scotland
Rating and Valuation Association
Association of Lands Valuation Assessors of Scotland
Association of Officers of the Ministry of Labour
Institute of Weights and Measures Administration
Institute of Baths Management
British Veterinary Association, Scottish Branch
Association of River Inspectors of Scotland
Institute of Burial and Cremation Administration
Association of Registrars of Scotland
Scottish Central Library
Scottish Library Association
Council for Museums and Galleries in Scotland
Scottish Federation of Museums and Art Galleries
Standing Commission on Museums and Galleries
Institute of Purchasing and Supply

EDINBURGH
HER MAJESTY'S STATIONERY OFFICE
1968

CONTENTS

SBN 11 490051 5

Memorandum by the
Stirling and Clackmannan Joint Police Board

1. The Stirling and Clackmannan Joint Police Board welcome the opportunity to submit evidence to the Royal Commission on Local Government in Scotland and beg to submit the following observations.

2. The Board is composed of 24 Members appointed by the Constituent Authorities. In view of the fact that each of the Constituent Authorities intend to submit evidence, either direct or through their appropriate association, the Board prefer to confine their evidence to recording their experiences as a Board in the execution of the duties delegated to them.

Constitution

3. In 1929 it so happened that Stirling County Council exercised the functions of Police Authority within the Burgh of Falkirk and, of course, this situation was continued thereafter. Shortly before the Second World War the County Council and Stirling Town Council combined for Police purposes and a Joint Committee was established covering the whole County.

4. In 1949 the Chief Constable of the combined force was due to retire and, as a consequence of some approaches made by the Scottish Home Department, consideration was given to the formation of a Board which would include the County of Clackmannan. After considerable discussion and negotiation, the Stirling and Clackmannan Joint Police Board was established by order of the Secretary of State on 12th May, 1949.

5. The composition of the Board provides for the appointment of 16 Members by Stirling County Council, of which 4 are Members of the County Council representing the Burgh of Falkirk; 4 are appointed by Stirling Town Council and 4 by Clackmannan County Council.

6. It is accepted generally that the decision to establish the Board serving this wide area has been successful and has promoted the build-up of an efficient organisation.

Functions

7. The Board are responsible for the exercise of the functions of the Constituent Authorities under the Police (Scotland) Acts.

8. During the lifetime of the Board there have been two Chief Constables.

9. The Chief Constable acts as Road Safety Organiser in Stirlingshire and members of the Police Force all participate in the work relating to Road Safety. He also acts as Chief Inspector for the purpose of the Diseases of Animals Acts and the members of the Force act as Inspectors.

10. The Board co-operates with the City of Glasgow and other adjoining Police Authorities in operating a Regional Crime Squad. The Board play their part in financing the Central Criminal Records Office and the Scottish Police College at Tulliallan.

Area

11. The area of the Board, which combines the geographical counties of Stirling and Clackmannan, is eminently manageable from the point of view of administration and contains a population of about 250,000.

Meetings

12. The Board meets monthly in Stirling and has appointed a Finance and General Purposes Committee, which also meets monthly. *Ad hoc* Sub-Committees are appointed from time to time to deal with special problems.

General

13. Having regard to the nature of the responsibilities devolving upon the Police Board it is possible that some advantage could be derived from organising the Police Service on a more regional basis but, at the same time, it is important, from the point of view of maintaining a close link between the Police and the general public, to ensure that a substantial measure of local control and interest is maintained.

November, 1966.

Memorandum by the
Dumfries and Galloway Police Committee

1. I refer to your letter inviting the Dumfries and Galloway Police Authority to submit evidence on the Commission's terms of reference.

2. The Dumfries and Galloway Police Committee are of the view that the present size of the Force and the area over which the Committee exercise their functions as Police Authority provides a viable and efficient unit for police purposes.

November, 1966.

Memorandum by the
Association of Scottish Police Superintendents

Judging from the views expressed recently at a meeting of the Executive Committee of this Association, it would appear that so far as local government functions are concerned, fewer problems exist in Force areas where there is only one local authority. This, so far as the Police are concerned, can only lead to one conclusion which is that wherever possible local authority and Force boundaries should coincide.

October, 1966.

Memorandum by the
Scottish Police Federation, Joint Central Committee

Introduction

1. The Scottish Police Federation has a membership of approximately 9,500 and represents all ranks of the Police Service in Scotland, up to and including chief inspector.

2. Since submitting evidence to the Royal Commission on the Police in 1960, the Federation's opinion has remained unchanged that consideration should be given to the advisability of the regionalisation or nationalisation of the Scottish Police Service. It was also the view of the Federation that police authorities had not availed themselves of the facilities for the voluntary amalgamation of police forces, and this has been further illustrated in the interim period by the example of Motherwell and Wishaw Constabulary and the Ayr Constabulary which could have been amalgamated with Lanarkshire and with Ayrshire. In both cases the posts of chief constable were filled despite the opportunity afforded.

3. To off-set this in some measure there has been voluntary amalgamation of Ross-shire and Sutherlandshire, now known as the Ross and Sutherland Constabulary. The counties of Perthshire and Kinross-shire have also combined with Perth City to provide the Perth and Kinross Constabulary.

Compulsory Amalgamations

4. The Federation welcomed the statement made by the Secretary of State for Scotland on 6th July, 1966, in the House of Commons, when he detailed his limited programme whereby the number of forces in Scotland would be reduced from thirty-one to twenty; these being:—

> (a) the county of Lanark and the burghs of Airdrie, Coatbridge, Hamilton and Motherwell and Wishaw;
>
> (b) the counties of Renfrew and Bute (already a combined area) and the burghs of Greenock and Paisley;
>
> (c) the county of Ayr and the burghs of Ayr and Kilmarnock;
>
> (d) the counties of Inverness and the burgh of Inverness; and
>
> (e) the counties of Caithness, Orkney and Shetland.

5. Apart from item (e), we had already envisaged the amalgamations outlined by the Secretary of State as a first, or natural step. Our identical recommendations were contained in a report dated 1st July, 1966, which was eventually submitted to the Secretary of State. It was intimated by the Secretary of State that he hoped for voluntary participation towards the creating of new combined areas outlined by him, but, should there be objections by any parties, he would use the powers granted to him to make any such amalgamation compulsory. Whilst we prepare this evidence to the Royal Commission on Local Government, we learn that at least one local authority is refusing to participate on a voluntary basis.

Further Amalgamations

6. In our report submitted to the Secretary of State we felt that Glasgow alone should remain a separate force although there could be a need for inclusion of surrounding districts, such as the burgh of Paisley, with the tidying of the boundary in general.

7. The only reason which could be advanced for Edinburgh continuing to operate as an individual unit was the fact of it being the capital city and should retain this distinction, but, in the general interest of efficiency, we felt that a natural amalgamation would be with the surrounding force of the Lothians and Peebles Constabulary.

8. It also followed that the city of Aberdeen could combine with the Scottish North-Eastern Counties Constabulary, while the city of Dundee could merge with the county of Angus. With amalgamation schemes being so topical at that time, it was with great regret and disappointment we learned that no advantage was to be taken by the vacancy created in the post of chief constable of the county of Angus to proceed with an amalgamation with Dundee city.

Amalgamation of County Areas

9. Having already envisaged the amalgamation of all the city and burgh forces, except for the City of Glasgow, we then considered the joining together of some of the remaining 18 forces:—

Orkney
Zetland
Caithness
Ross and Sutherland
Inverness-shire
Perth and Kinross
Angus
Scottish N.E. Counties
Argyll
Ayrshire
Lanarkshire
Fife
Stirling and Clackmannan
Dunbartonshire
Renfrew and Bute
Lothians and Peebles
Berwick, Roxburgh and Selkirk
Dumfries and Galloway

10. As a result of our deliberations, we recommended to the Secretary of State that Lanarkshire could well remain a force on its own. This was also our recommendation for:—

Scottish N.E. Counties
Fife
Renfrew and Bute

11. We also recommended that the following forces could form combined constabularies:—

(a) Orkney: Zetland: Caithness: Ross and Sutherland: Inverness-shire.

The Royal Commission on Local Government may wish to give consideration to our view that the entire Hebrides should come within the jurisdiction of this combined force. The Isle of Mull, which is at present part of Argyll, could also be part of this force.

Moray and Nairn, which at present forms part of the Scottish N.E. Counties Group, might well be detached and joined to the combined area. This would lend towards a better division of areas.

We suggested an alternative proposal for Orkney whereby it could be joined with the Scottish North-Eastern Counties Constabulary. This was also the wish of the Orkney

Branch Board of the Police Federation who had in mind the existing administration connections with Aberdeen in relation to the Hospitals, Fire Board and Aberdeen Prison.

(*b*) Perth and Kinross: Angus.

We consider that Kinross-shire should no longer form part of the Perth and Kinross force, but instead should be linked with Fife as the larger part of it lies within the more natural boundary of Fife.

(*c*) Stirling and Clackmannan: Dunbartonshire: Argyll.

We suggest that Clackmannan could merge with Fife instead of being joined with Stirlingshire as at present. Argyll could extend its boundary to include islands such as Arran, and also taking in Bute, which at present form parts of the Renfrew and Bute force.

The Federation would view Renfrewshire linking with Ayrshire.

(*d*) Dumfries and Galloway: Ayrshire.

An initial step could provide for the amalgamation of these two forces, and this was suggested to the Secretary of State. Our further proposal, which we would put to the Commission, is that the Dumfries and Galloway force could be divided so that Galloway merges with Ayrshire (plus Renfrewshire as suggested at (*c*) above), while Dumfries would link up with Lanarkshire.

12. Many of our suggestions are mainly dictated by reason of responsibility for the policing of the arterial roads running through the combined areas. We have also had our thoughts directed towards Regions and have taken cognisance of the Zones applicable to Civil Defence operations which are closely linked to that of the Police Service. In the event of hostilities it would be natural, to facilitate matters, to adopt the Civil Defence pattern of 3 Zones to be known as Regions. The forces within these Regions, and already within the Zone plan of Civil Defence, are:—

    (*a*) Northern Region

        Orkney
        Zetland
        Caithness
        Ross and Sutherland
        Inverness
        Inverness-shire
        Perth and Kinross
        Fife
        Angus
        Dundee
        Aberdeen
        Scottish N.E. Counties

    (*b*) Western Region

        Kilmarnock
        Ayr
        Ayrshire
        Glasgow
        Lanarkshire
        Airdrie
        Hamilton
        Coatbridge
        Motherwell and Wishaw
        Stirling and Clackmannan

Dunbartonshire
Paisley
Greenock
Renfrew and Bute
Argyll
Dumfries and Galloway

(c) Eastern Region

Edinburgh
Lothians and Peebles
Berwick, Roxburgh and Selkirk.

Local Government

13. The exercise of local government functions within the existing structure of local authorities has, in general, been quite good, but there is always the tendency to lean towards economy rather than efficiency on the part of some police authorities. Central Government, on the basis of the present police system, is responsible for the payment of the Exchequer grant, without which forces could not in practice be maintained. This grant is at the rate of 50% of the approved expenditure of a police authority and is conditional on the Secretary of State being satisfied that the area for which the authority is responsible is efficiently policed and gives him power to withhold the grant in whole or in part if he is not satisfied on this point.

14. It has for long been the opinion of the Federation that the burden of 50% on local rates is too heavy and should be reduced to 25%. We can see no reason why the police can not be placed on a similar financial basis as the Civil Defence. The existing arrangement leads to the anomaly that the police may require a wireless set for Civil Defence purposes. Central Government grant would then be 75%. If the identical wireless set was required for police purposes then the grant would only be 50%. It is therefore perfectly obvious that it is much easier to obtain equipment for civil defence purposes than it is to receive sanction from the local authority in order to secure equipment for police use.

Courts

15. It is likely that alteration to the existing local authority boundaries will affect the areas of jurisdiction for which courts are at present responsible.

16. If it is possible for the Royal Commission to deal with this point under its terms of reference, the Federation would ask that consideration be given to our request that lay magistrates should not be persons who are solicitors with criminal practices, licence holders, or members of the staff of newspapers.

October, 1966.

Memorandum by the
Central Fire Area Joint Committee

1. The Central Fire Area Joint Committee welcome the opportunity to submit evidence to the Royal Commission on Local Government in Scotland and beg to submit the following observations.

2. The Joint Committee is composed of 17 Members appointed by the Constituent Authorities who are the Counties of Stirling, Dunbarton and Clackmannan and the Burghs of Stirling, Falkirk, Clydebank and Dumbarton. The County Councils each appoint three Members and the Burghs each appoint two Members. The Chairman and Vice-Chairman may not be appointed from the same authority. In view of the fact that each of the Constituent Authorities intend to submit evidence either direct or through their appropriate association, the Joint Committee prefer to confine their evidence to recording their experiences in the execution of the duties delegated to them.

Functions

3. The responsibilities devolving on the Joint Committee are those assigned to local authorities under the Fire Services Act, 1947.

4. These duties comprise the administration of the Fire Service within the area of the three Counties and, of course, the Burghs, the provision of Fire Stations on a whole-time and retained basis, the provision of the necessary appliances and equipment and the appointment of a Firemaster with the appropriate establishment of whole-time and retained personnel.

5. In addition to the duties of fire fighting, the Joint Committee have responsibilities regarding Fire Prevention, the inspection of premises and the issue of certificates under the Factories Act and the Offices, Shops and Railway Premises Act.

Area

6. The area served by the Central Area Fire Brigade was fixed having regard to experiences gained under the National Fire Service during the war.

7. The Headquarters of the Brigade are situated in Kirkintilloch and there are two fairly clearly defined areas of higher fire risk (First) in the Eastern part—the area from Cumbernauld to Grangemouth with the industrial development including the oil refinery and associated plastics industry—and (Second) in the Western part—Clydeside and the Vale of Leven.

8. While it is not necessarily the most convenient unit for purposes of administration this arrangement has worked efficiently and in general to the satisfaction of the Constituent Authorities.

9. There have been difficulties of wireless communication to overcome due to geographical features but these have been solved and there is, of course, the physical problem of transport between Clydeside and the rest of the area due to the fact that the most direct route lies through the City of Glasgow.

Meetings, etc.

10. The Central Fire Area Joint Committee was established in 1948. Meetings are held monthly, alternately in Glasgow and in Stirling. This arrangement was made to suit the convenience of the Members for the Western part of the area.

11. The Joint Committee have appointed a Property and General Purposes Sub-Committee, consisting of one Member from each authority, which meets as required and, on average, about five times a year.

12. The Joint Committee on one occasion in the year—usually about the month of August—carry out an inspection of Fire Brigade properties in one or other parts of their area of administration. This enables the Members to become familiar with the geographical features and problems associated with the various parts of the area of which they may have no direct knowledge.

General

13. The main complaint which is heard from Members relates to the amount of grant which is forthcoming for the Service from treasury funds. The Joint Committee is frequently subjected to criticism from the Constituent Authorities on the matter of the cost of maintaining the Fire Service.

14. The Constitution of the Joint Committee provides that the Annual Estimates of the Joint Committee must receive approval of the Constituent Authorities. Failure on the part of an authority to approve can and does lead to difficulties in administration. Expenditure which may be proposed and which is not provided for in the Annual Estimates also requires the specific approval of the Constituent Authorities, who often express their concern at the rising cost of the Fire Service by withholding approval.

15. There is, of course, machinery for dealing with the situation by reference to the Secretary of State, who acts as an arbiter, but the fact that this situation does arise is an indication of the concern of the Constituent Authorities at the cost of the Fire Service.

16. While the present arrangement works satisfactorily, it must be appreciated that the incidence of fires recognises no boundaries and Mutual Aid Arrangements exist with all adjoining Brigades. It is for consideration whether the Fire Service might not be better organised on a regional basis covering even wider areas than the present Fire Areas.

November, 1966.

Memorandum by the
Chief Fire Officers' Association

1. The Chief Fire Officers' Association was formed in 1947 to allow membership by Chief Fire Officers and Firemasters covered by the Fire Services Act, 1947. All Chief Fire Officers in England and Wales and Firemasters in Scotland are members of the Association.

2. The management of the Association is by a Council which comprises one representative from each district of the Association and three National Representatives. The Association has representatives sitting on all the Committees of the Central Fire Brigades Advisory Councils for England and Wales and Scotland. Association representatives are members of a wide variety of Committees of Central Government Departments, Industry, Insurance and Local Authorities. Members of the Association, in their own right, act as advisers to the Scottish Employers' Associations, County Councils Association and the Association of Municipal Corporations.

3. Ministerial responsibility for fire-fighting functions is vested in the Secretary of State for Scotland and in 1948, when responsibility for the Fire Service was restored to Local Authorities by the Fire Services Act, 1947, the decision was made in Scotland to group Local Authorities together into Joint Committees each with a single Brigade, with the exception of Glasgow, where the Town Council of the City is the responsible Authority. Outside of Glasgow, ten areas were set up, each administered by a Joint Committee representative of the Council of the Counties and the large Burghs in the area.

4. The Association has taken a close look at the working of the Fire Service and the viability of the areas of command. Our conclusions are:

(1) That the Fire Service should operate at a level not below the top tier of Local Government but, should it be necessary for operational command reasons, and in the light of our observations on the minimum size of commands as outlined in paragraph 3, to have a system of combination or joint schemes. we consider, on balance, that combination schemes are the more satisfactory method.

(2) Local Authority control of the Service by elected representatives should continue.

(3) (a) Communications, both roads and telephone exchange areas, are important to Fire Service operations. We do not consider that there should be island areas within a geographical fire area or a series of telephone exchange areas. These areas should be covered by combination schemes if the new local government organisation does not overcome the difficulty. Experience shows that the interests of the public are best served when a fire in a high risk area is attended by men and appliances from one command, though it is appreciated that there will be boundaries between the commands and the nearest fire appliance should always attend the fire.

(b) A command structure should be of sufficient size to establish that the posts of commanders will attract sufficient numbers of the right type of recruit for the commanders of the future. Each command should be large enough to justify a comprehensive staff covering the following specialist functions:

   (i) Transport;
   (ii) Recruitment and Training;
   (iii) Water;
   (iv) Communications and Mobilising;
   (v) Fire Prevention;
   (vi) Emergency Planning;
   (vii) Administrative Staff.

13

Each specialist function should have sufficient Officers to allow for promotion within the sections. All present Fire Authority areas do not have staff on this basis, thus seriously affecting the promotional outlook of the Service.

(c) The majority of the Firemasters in Scotland consider the present 11 commands to be satisfactory, but they do not measure, in all cases, to the requirements stated above. During the last war there were fewer commands in Scotland and the Association view is that eleven commands are too many, despite the unusual geographical and population problems.

(4) There should be an investigation into the possibility that the Service should include all armed forces fire services, all Governmental Departments handling fire service matters and airports, but should not include industrial fire brigades.

(5) Trade Unions, with political affinities and pressures at certain levels, are not suitable for a professional Service like the Fire Service. A federation would be more appropriate. The present method of reaching agreement at N.J.C. level and the subsequent implementation by Fire Authorities does not allow for the economic use of manpower.

(6) All fire prevention statutes are aimed at preserving life from fire. This aspect must be expanded to include the protection of structures and contents and, until this is done, it is not likely that we shall make a major impact on rising fire loss. A consolidating Act is required for fire service legislation.

(7) The Service should cover all types of rescue work at accidents and emergencies where human life is involved, and the Service responsibility should be defined by legislation.

March, 1967.

Memorandum by the
Fire Brigades Union

1. It would not be the purpose of the Fire Brigades Union to make comment on the future structure of Local Government in Scotland as such. It is in respect of the organisation and administration of the Fire Service as a local government service that the Union directs the attention of the Royal Commission.

2. The present organisation of the Fire Service in Scotland comprises 11 Fire Boards, as follows:—

(i) ANGUS: County of Angus and City of Dundee
873 sq. miles   Pop.   280,600   R.V. £5,767,000

(ii) CENTRAL SCOTLAND: Counties of Clackmannan, Dunbarton, Stirling and burghs therein
1,800 sq. miles   Pop.   434,200   R.V. £10,494,754

(iii) FIFE: County of Fife including large burghs of Kirkcaldy and Dunfermline
508 sq. miles   Pop.   323,229   R.V. £6,407,760

(iv) GLASGOW: City of Glasgow
62 sq. miles   Pop. 1,029,147   R.V. £21,214,108

(v) LANARKSHIRE: County of Lanarkshire
837 sq. miles   Pop.   581,744   R.V. £10,613,530

(vi) NORTH EASTERN SCOTLAND: Counties of Aberdeen, Banff and Kincardine and the joint county of Moray and Nairn and the county of the city of Aberdeen
3,622 sq. miles   Pop.   451,240   R.V. £7,699,233

(vii) NORTHERN SCOTLAND: Inverness-shire, Ross-shire, Sutherland, Caithness, Orkney and Shetland
10,965 sq. miles   Pop.   218,371

(viii) PERTH AND KINROSS: Counties of Perth and Kinross and City of Perth
2,560 sq. miles   Pop.   133,722   R.V. £2,414,754

(ix) SOUTH EASTERN SCOTLAND: City of Edinburgh, Counties of Berwick, East Lothian, Midlothian, Peebles, Roxburgh, Selkirk and West Lothian
2,500 sq. miles   Pop.   840,830   R.V. £18,361,364

(x) SOUTH WESTERN SCOTLAND: Counties of Ayr, Dumfries, Kirkcudbright and Wigtown, and the Burghs of Ayr, Kilmarnock and Dumfries
3,600 sq. miles   Pop.   492,873   R.V. £8,728,899

(xi) WESTERN SCOTLAND: Counties of Renfrew, Argyll and Bute and the large burghs of Paisley, Greenock and Port Glasgow
3,553 sq. miles   Pop.   422,805   R.V. £7,842,325

3. A great deal of unnecessary duplication in the Fire Service arises as a consequence of multiple units separately organised and administered. During the period of the National Fire Service, 1941–1948, the Fire Service in Scotland was in fact one single regional unit and as such worked successfully. The Union submits that the Fire Service in Scotland should be administered either by a single regional Scottish Fire Service or that the present joint Fire Boards should be greatly reduced in number and expanded in size. It is necessary in the nature of the Fire Service that all the best type of equipment and most efficient techniques in both fire fighting and training should be in use in every Brigade. Therefore the Fire Service requires the highest degree of standardisation in every aspect including its financial base.

4. It is chiefly at Local Government Boundary areas where operational overlap exists in the Fire Service both by way of attendance at incidents and in the distribution of special appliances and equipment. To reduce the number of boundaries would consequently reduce the extent of this overlap. The overlap in Fire Service communications arrangements is notorious. A regional type Fire Service would eliminate this overlap. In any event the Fire Service should operate a single regional linked radio frequency.

5. In the field of Fire Prevention it is most important that activities are greatly increased based on a code of standard practices, built up on pooled experiences. This desirable achievement is impeded firstly by the many differing local arrangements made by local authorities in the structure and organisation of Fire Prevention measures which, in some cases, excludes the Fire Service from the more important aspects of this work; secondly, because there is no real central control and guidance in this branch of fire engineering and, thirdly, because men on Fire Stations are with a few exceptions excluded from this area of Fire Service activity. Regional Fire Prevention meetings already take place usually attended by the designated senior Fire Prevention Officer in each Brigade. The influence and activities of Fire Prevention measures could be greatly strengthened through a Regional type Fire Service.

6. The Fire Service today, in addition to fire fighting and fire prevention duties, is more and more called on to provide other emergency rescue services particularly at road accidents. The number of road accidents attended by the Fire Service in Scotland is now in the region of 2,000 annually. It therefore follows that the maximum co-ordination and standard equipment and training is required. This is better achieved by the creation of fewer Brigades larger in size.

7. Although the Fire Brigades Union does not advocate the nationalisation of the Fire Service, the Union considers that the Service requires the strongest links with central government through the Scottish Home and Health Department.

8. It must be the Government's overall responsibility to ensure that Britain's Fire Services are modern and efficient. For this reason the Union holds the view strongly that the Fire Service should be lifted out of the local government block grant financial arrangements and become subject to a direct Government grant of 50% of the costs. Thus, elevating the administration of this vital life saving Service above local political considerations.

9. For the reasons set out above the Union therefore urges that the Scottish Fire Service should be organised on the basis of a single regional unit, or alternatively, the present 11 joint Fire Boards be greatly reduced to certainly no more than half that number.

October, 1966.

Memorandum by the
Association of Civil Defence Officers, Scottish Region

1. The Members of the Scottish Region of the Association of Civil Defence Officers are pleased and honoured to have the opportunity of contributing to the deliberations of the Royal Commission on Local Government in Scotland. In the submission of the following evidence to the Commission, they have kept in mind its terms of reference and, within the scope of those terms of reference, have concentrated their conclusions, as requested, on the desirability of providing the Commission with:

(a) evidence of any practical difficulties which have been experienced in the exercise of local governments functions (in this case Civil Defence) within the existing structure of local authorities; and

(b) positive suggestions for reform.

2. At the outset it has had to be accepted that the changes in the Central Government's policy for Civil Defence, resulting from the recent Review of Civil Defence Preparations, contain considerable inference of a reorganisation of the Service at local authority level. However, as the detailed nature of this reorganisation is unknown at the date of submitting this Memorandum, the evidence set out below is based on the administration of Civil Defence at local authority level as it exists at present.

3. In putting the Commission's request to the Members of the Region for consideration, the Executive of the Region deemed it advisable, particularly in order to assist Members in marshalling their facts along the lines desired by the Commission, to carry out a further analysis of items 1(a) and (b) above, on the following bases:—

(a) Are the Civil Defence functions of local authorities correctly defined and properly distributed?

(b) Is the extent of territory over which these functions are exercised too big, too small or just about right?

(c) How should Civil Defence, as a local authority function, be fitted into local government as a whole, bearing in mind the need to reduce committees to a minimum?

(d) If the office of Clerk to the authority is replaced (in the event of Regionalisation) by some corresponding office, is any consequential change needed in the appointment designated "Civil Defence Commissioner"?

(e) What should be the division of responsibility between local authority officials and elected members?

4. It is generally agreed that the Civil Defence functions of local authorities are correctly defined by statute. Nevertheless, while these (war-time) functions are mainly extensions in some form of existing peace-time local authority services, many authorities seem to have lost sight of the necessity of placing responsibility for the planning for the function in peace-time and the carrying of it out in war, on the Departments (and in consequence their Chief Officials) responsible for the services in peace-time, e.g. Emergency Feeding to the School Meals Service. The biggest single factor contributing to a lack of progress on the part of most local authorities to plan for war, is in the training of their staffs in Civil Defence to the extent required to enable those staffs to carry out the tasks necessary for the continuance of the services of the local authority in war.

5. While Regulations made under the Civil Defence Act, 1948, empower the appropriate Minister to direct local authorities to "train suitable members of their staff"—and from time to time the Minister has exercised this power to a degree—local authorities have not

17

generally succeeded in obtaining the co-operation of their staffs to take Civil Defence training. From the voluntary point of view, it has been found that by far the majority of local authority staff are reluctant to take the required training, due it is felt, to an actual (or feigned) unawareness of its relevance to their normal occupation. To some extent it can be reasoned that members of local authority staff put a wrong construction on the functions of the Civil Defence Corps by assuming that its members will "take over" in war-time, whereas the actual role of the Corps is only to assist local authorities in carrying out their war-time functions.

6. As regards the extent of territory over which Civil Defence functions are exercised, this is dependent on three particular factors, i.e. communications, the size of the area and the population of the area, insofar as these remain compatible with the efficient administration of Civil Defence in its peculiarly parochial nature. The present system of grouping two or more authorities, broadly-speaking as so many "Civil Defence Areas" working to a "parent "Group Control within the operational framework of a Zone, would appear generally to have taken account of these factors satisfactorily. There are, however, a minority of cases where a slight variation of the existing organisation would be to advantage, e.g. by the resiting of Group Controls; the inclusion in the Group(s) of the large Burghs in a County, or the transfer of an Area from its present Group to a Group adjacent.

7. While, as has been indicated, the system is generally satisfactory in principle from the point of view of the operational organisation in the life-saving phase, central government policy indications for the future tend toward a lessening of emphasis on that phase in favour of maximum effort on the later phases of survival, recovery and restoration. In these circumstances, and in the interests of increased efficiency of administration during the equally important peace-time planning and preparatory phase, Civil Defence in all its aspects would be better served by the amalgamation of the authorities concerned under one joint committee, rather than their being grouped under a co-ordinating committee.

8. By virtue of the statutory obligation on local authorities to set up a Civil Defence service, it merits its place alongside all the other services which local authorities are required to maintain, with one essential difference. Civil Defence by its very nature impinges on virtually every one of the more "conventional" services of the local authority, thereby requiring an important degree of participation by those chief officials of all Departments responsible for the administration of such services, to produce plans for their extension and/or continuance under the canopy of "Civil Defence" in war. In most local authorities, the lack of positive action in this direction presents a major difficulty to those Officers appointed by the authority to be responsible for the detailed administration of Civil Defence.

9. In view of the fore-going, it follows that the Civil Defence Committee of an authority must be representative of those Committees already responsible for defining local policy in relation to such of its peace-time services as will, by their extension/continuance in war, make an essential contribution to the survival of the community. It is only by the existence of a Civil Defence Committee so constituted that an authority can ensure that the central government's policy directions for Civil Defence are being fully implemented.

10. The Clerk to the authority, being responsible for *inter alia*, the co-ordination of the efforts of all local authority services, it is axiomatic that he do likewise in relation to the administration of Civil Defence, the Civil Defence Officer being responsible to him for the day-to-day ground work of collating Departmental war plans and the conduct of Civil Defence training. While it is essential that the Civil Defence Officer should have direct access to Heads of Departments in relation to matters affecting the planning of their services for war, in the final analysis it is the Clerk to the authority only, by virtue of his office, who is in a position to give directions on the basis of local policy made by the appropriate Committee.

11. The present general procedure in Civil Defence Groups for the allocation of responsibility for the conduct of Civil Defence operations is:—

(a) To appoint a Civil Defence Controller to be responsible during the strictly life-saving phase, selection being made from either of the following:—

   (i) a person of suitable military background, with or without experience of local government;

   (ii) a Senior Elected Member; or

   (iii) a Senior Official of an authority, e.g. the Clerk.

(b) To replace the Controller by a Civil Defence Commissioner, at the conclusion of the life-saving phase, to take charge during the subsequent survival, recovery and restoration phases. The choice of Commissioner has almost exclusively fallen upon a Senior Elected Member, the assumption being that, while the life-saving phase is a quasi-military operation, survival, recovery and restoration are essentially concerned with the machinery of local government, requiring to be conducted by a person from the hierarchy of that organisation.

12. As has already been mentioned elsewhere in this Memorandum, the trend of Central Government policy in relation to the conduct of Civil Defence operations demonstrates a decrease in the time and emphasis hitherto given to the life-saving phase, compensated by a distinct increase in the importance placed on survival, recovery and restoration. Accepting the fact that a necessary qualification for leadership in those later phases is knowledge and experience of local government, it is considered self-evident that the appointment of Civil Defence Group Commissioner should be held by the expert in that field, namely the Clerk to the authority (or his equivalent in the event of Regionalisation of local government). It is further recommended that, because of the apparent limitation of time and emphasis to be placed on the life-saving phase in the future, the appointment of Group Commissioner should include responsibility for the function presently carried out by the Civil Defence Group Controller, i.e. control of operations during the life-saving phase.

13. In order to achieve efficient planning and co-ordination of the efforts of all the Civil Defence Areas within a Group, throughout all phases of operations, it is suggested that, from the remaining Clerks to the authorities (or other suitable members of their staffs) of those Areas, there be appointed an appropriate number of Civil Defence Area Controllers, each responsible in his particular Area, working to the Civil Defence Group Commissioner, for the furtherance of Civil Defence planning in peace-time and the conduct of operations in war. Acceptance of this degree of responsibility by Clerks to authorities would tend to provide a lead for other Chief Officials, as doubtless each Clerk in his role of Civil Defence Group Commissioner and/or Civil Defence Area Controller, would gather around him his Heads of Departments and delegate responsibility as necessary.

14. In peace-time, local authority officials must be made aware of their Civil Defence responsibilities and carry out the necessary preparations in relation to the services administered by them, for the putting of those services on a war footing. Where it is necessary for an authority to appoint officers to take charge of specific responsibilities in war, e.g. Billeting, Care of the Homeless, Emergency Feeding, etc., the appointments should be given to and be wholly accepted by those Chief Officials whose Departments provide equivalent, or closely associated services in peace-time.

15. Elected Members must exercise the same function in relation to Civil Defence as a local authority service as they do to the other services of the Local Authority (Regulation 1 of the Civil Defence (General) (Scotland) Regulations, 1949). It is suggested, however, that the responsibility of Elected Members need not necessarily be required to go beyond that of the formulation of policy, into the purely functional field of Civil Defence.

16. To summarise the main points in particular:—

(a) The Civil Defence functions of local authorities are, in general, correctly defined but inadequately delegated. Statutory measures, directed specifically at the training of local authority staff in Civil Defence, are essential if the authorities' services are to be efficiently geared to war-time commitments.

(b) The grouping/amalgamation (or Regionalisation) of local authorities is practicable, provided it is commensurate with efficient communications; the size of the area and the distribution of its population, having regard to the peculiarly parochial nature of the functions of Civil Defence. In the interests of efficiency of administration, this suggests that amalgamation of authorities under a joint committee is preferable to that of grouping for purely operational purposes under a co-ordinating committee.

(c) The fact that Civil Defence is applicable, to a greater or lesser extent to all peace-time services of the local authority, a situation imposed on authorities by statute, makes it essential that it be given its rightful place, in the Scheme of Administration of every local authority, as a Service, headed by the Civil Defence Officer, working to the Clerk to the authority and with the appropriate Heads of Departments, for the collation of Departmental war plans and the conduct of Civil Defence training.

(d) In the allocation of responsibility for the co-ordination of all phases of operations within a Civil Defence Group, it is recommended that the Clerk to the Group Authority be appointed Civil Defence Group Commissioner and that, from the remaining Clerks of the authorities (or other suitable members of their staffs) within the Group, an appropriate number of Civil Defence Area Controllers be appointed to work to the Group Commissioner for the peace-time planning of the Areas' services in war and their subsequent control in operations.

(e) The Civil Defence responsibility of local authority officials, and in particular Heads of Departments, is that of formulating the necessary plans and other preparations for the extension/continuance, in war, of the services for which they are responsible in peace-time. Furthermore, when additional services or functions, required to be provided for in war by an authority, are considered to be relevant or appropriate to particular peace-time services or functions, the Officials responsible for these in peace-time, must be required to include the planning/preparations for those additional services/functions within the compass of their peace-time responsibilities.

(f) While it is constitutionally essential that Elected Members be responsible for deciding local policy for the implementation of the Central Government's intentions for Civil Defence (as is their prerogative in regard to all other local authority services), it is suggested that their participation—just as in the case of those other services—need not necessarily be extended into the purely functional field of Civil Defence.

October, 1966.

Memorandum by the
Local Government Auditors' (Scotland) Association

1. The Local Government Auditors' (Scotland) Association has been invited by the Royal Commission on Local Government in Scotland to submit evidence bearing on the terms of reference and, in particular, to provide:—

    (a) evidence of any practical difficulties which have been experienced in the exercise of local government functions within the existing structure of local authorities, and

    (b) positive suggestions for reform.

2. The Local Government Auditors' (Scotland) Association submits that, in the existing structure of local authorities, a serious accounting difficulty is experienced in the smaller units where, owing to the total accounting staff of the authority being so small numerically, no proper system of internal check on cash and other records is possible.

3. This position becomes more serious where the responsible financial officer is employed on a part-time basis and is not constantly at hand to supervise more junior staff.

4. That this is a serious practical problem for the smaller authorities is evidenced by the fact that in practically all cases where a defalcation occurs it is in a small unit where it has not been possible to have an adequate separation of duties so as to give a reasonable system of internal check.

5. The existence of a large number of small authorities results in wasteful duplication of financial arrangements. In the small authority the chief financial officer may well be capable of discharging greater responsibilities than those required of him. Alternatively, in order to keep down the cost of administration, a chief financial officer may be employed who is inadequately qualified to discharge his responsibilities in full.

6. Late presentation of the Annual Abstract of Accounts to the Auditor and to the Scottish Development Department occurs and this is attributed partially to inadequate staffing and partially to the volume of detail required in the form of accounts. It has been noticed that a common factor in many cases of defalcations has been the failure to complete Accounts timeously.

7. Local Government Auditors' (Scotland) Association suggest that the difficulties set out in paragraphs 2, 3 and 4 can only be met if the size of individual units is increased by the amalgamation of a number of smaller authorities. The delays referred to in paragraph 4 could be mitigated if some simplification of the form of the Annual Abstract of Accounts was allowed to small authorities.

Memorandum by the
Institute of Chartered Accountants of Scotland

1. The Council of The Institute of Chartered Accountants of Scotland understands that the Royal Commission on Local Government in Scotland would welcome evidence bearing on the Commission's terms of reference and in particular as regards:—

   (a) any practical difficulties which have been experienced in the exercise of local government functions within the existing structure of local authorities; and

   (b) positive suggestions for reform.

2. The trend in modern business is towards larger units leading to greater efficiency and economy. It is obvious that specialised activities, such as finance, require the services of qualified and specialised staffs to administer them in the most efficient manner. The Council would urge that, in the consideration of possible regroupings of local authorities or revision of the various powers entrusted to them, regard should be had to the commercial considerations which could be usefully applied in many instances. In particular the Council would suggest that there should be a centralisation of financial arrangements especially in rural areas. Thus, although small burghs might continue to prepare their individual budgets, the actual administration of assessments and rate collection could be done more efficiently by the county council.

3. The centralising of rate collection is but one of many activities which the Council feels should be considered with a view to achieving economy and efficiency. Preparation of payrolls comes immediately to mind, but there must be many other instances—such as those involving bulk orders for supplies and equipment where centralised buying policies could save money.

4. There are a large number of special grant claims logded each year with the Secretary of State. The preparation of these claims must inevitably involve the expenditure of a considerable amount of time by staff of local authorities. Whilst it is appreciated that numerous claims may be necessary for completely new projects it is felt that there is some case for extending the range of block grants to certain items of expenditure, e.g. education and police.

5. There is one relatively minor anomaly—as it seems to the Council—to which the Royal Commission's attention is invited: this is the procedure whereby in special districts of county councils there are individual amenity assessments in respect of such matters as sewerage, lighting and water. It might be thought more suitable—and possibly economic—that these special assessments should be abolished and the rateable value of the property adjusted to take account of whatever amenities are available in each case.

6. The Council has had the opportunity of considering the memorandum submitted by the Local Government Auditors Association to the Royal Commission and is in complete agreement with the views expressed in that memorandum.

Memorandum by the
Rating and Valuation Association

1. Founded in 1882, the Association's membership includes central and local government officers engaged in rating, valuation for rating and valuation for other purposes, valuers in private practice and with public boards, and clerks of local valuation panels. Its main objects are to keep its members informed, to undertake research, to publish information about rating and valuation and related matters and to arrange examinations as a test of knowledge for professional membership. It functions through an elected council of 28 members, a headquarters staff, regional technical groups and area branches; its membership is 3,400.

2. The Royal Commission's terms of reference are:—

> To consider the structure of local government in Scotland in relation to its existing functions; and to make recommendations for authorities and boundaries, and for functions and their division, having regard to the size and character of areas in which these can be most effectively exercised and the need to sustain a viable system of local democracy.

3. If it is necessary, in order to satisfy these tests of effectiveness, viability and democratic functioning, to create large regional units of local government, then bearing in mind the great diversity of different parts of the country in terms of population, communications, economic activity and the financial resources of inhabitants, the Association submits that:—Democratically elected regional authorities should be appointed, each regional authority should study its geographical and population factors and create its own pattern of second-tier authorities. There should be adequate finance, based on local and regional revenue resources and central government funds. The areas of regional authorities will have to be determined by Parliament.

4. The creation of regions by the simple process of amalgamating existing county council areas may be thought rational. The Association submits that the first administrative step might be the appointment of a regional assembly, comprising representatives from each existing local authority in the regional area concerned, together with members of Parliament representing constituencies within the same area. This assembly could then carry out the necessary electoral processes either by way of the election of individual candidates at local elections or, less democratically, by permitting each constituent existing local authority to appoint members of the regional council on a fair population basis. On balance the advantages are thought to lie with the local election procedure, particularly as this will assist the maintenance of truly democratic local government.

5. While the newly elected regional council sets about the second stage of the work of local government reorganisation—the creation of second-tier authorities in their area— the existing local authorities would continue to function as before.

6. In this way the risks which had to be taken when London government was re-shaped within the limits of a tight time-table, can be avoided. A more leisurely appraisal of public needs in terms of the number, size, finance and functions of second-tier authorities will be possible. Some final date will have to be fixed for the submission by each region of their schemes for Parliamentary approval, but a generous time-table will make possible a complementary inquiry into revenue resources, for local and regional purposes, in the light of overall national taxation sources and limits.

7. The division of functions between regions and local authorities will necessarily depend on national policies as well as regional preferences. For example, the creation of regions may well justify reconsideration of present responsibilities. Hospital, gas, water

and electricity boards might conceivably be absorbed by regional councils, and far greater public goodwill may be one advantage from bringing these within democratic electoral processes.

8. The present system of valuation for rating in Scotland as revised by the Valuation and Rating (Scotland) Act, 1956 has proved to be satisfactory. Attached to this memorandum is an appendix in which the rating system is considered and particular reference is made to valuation problems in paragraph 41 to 44.

9. The division of what are at present local government functions may have to be the subject of some central directive. As a matter of policy it may be thought necessary to place the prime responsibility for town and country planning, police, major roads and education with the regional authorities, subject only to the right to a reasonable degree of delegation where local circumstances warrant this. So far as other functions are concerned it may be found in some regions that all can be effectively undertaken by the second-tier authorities, their areas, population and financial resources justifying this.

10. However, in more sparsely populated regions, for example, the size and area of second-tier authorities will vary widely. Correspondingly, the regional councils must have freedom themselves to undertake certain of these residual functions, in whole or in part. Essentially the pattern of local government should fit the varying needs of each region.

Finance of Local Government

11. Finance is, inevitably, the most decisive factor in determining the degree of independence for regional and local authorities.

12. Minimum standards of services must be reconciled with independent functioning. This will entail the continuance of some form of central government subvention, but it is to be hoped that the finance of second-tier authorities can be so arranged that the minimum of central government funds, and consequential control, will be the aim.

13. It is arguable that the only really necessary central government money is that required to finance regional services. The Association suggests that in the light of any recommendations of the Royal Commission on boundaries and functions it may emerge that to supplement the rating system untried and hitherto rejected sources of revenue may well be investigated in depth. The Association will very gladly give any assistance it can in any research necessary.

The Rating System

14. Local rates constitute an expenditure tax. This year the sum likely to be collected in the United Kingdom is approximately £1,500 million. It is surely academic to suggest dismantling an existing revenue producing tax of this order when our overall taxation needs are so pressing, and when taxation trends are away from further taxes on incomes and towards increased expenditure taxes.

15. Attached to this memorandum is an appendix on the nature of rates, the validity of the basis of assessment, the advantages of the system and the criticisms applied to it.

16. Rating is based on principle rather than some arbitrary basis and this attribute is of incalculable value from a taxation standpoint. The basis of assessment for local rates—the annual value of properties—is directly related to the local government services provided from the rate revenue as shown in paragraphs 5 to 25 of the appendix.

17. In those paragraphs it is shown that rates are a tax on accommodation, accommodation benefits from local government services, accommodation adds to the costs of local services, and the value of accommodation is created and maintained by those services.

The Association submits that the rating system, suitably adjusted from time to time to meet prevailing circumstances, will conveniently provide most of the finance necessary to sustain the second-tier local authorities envisaged in the foregoing recommendations.

18. There are criticisms of the rating system, but none disclose major defects incapable of an effective remedy. There are considerable advantages in the system relating to reasonable financial independence of local authorities, relative simplicity, cheap and effective collection, certainty and predictability of yield and, not least, productivity. On any proposal to abolish rating the Association submits there should be a most careful appraisal of its advantages, the ready means of correcting admitted deficiencies and, not least, the economic and social effects of abolition bearing in mind the necessity for alternative equivalent revenue and the effect of abolition on property values.

November, 1966.

Appendix

EVIDENCE ON THE RATING SYSTEM

Nature of Rates

1. Rates are one of the oldest forms of taxation in this country. The poor rate from which the present general rate has evolved originated in the sixteenth century. Rates have ousted virtually all other forms of local taxation (including incidentally their predecessor for poor rate purposes—ability to pay) and have survived and developed into the fundamental source of local revenue (apart from grants) because of their intrinsic simplicity, their ease and economy of levy and collection and their ready yield.

2. Rates have always been charged at so much in the £ on the annual value or net letting value of houses, buildings and land. An outline of the history of rating in Scotland is given in Appendix A of the Report of the Scottish Valuation and Rating Committee, 1954 (Sorn Committee) Cmd. 9244.

3. Formerly the incidence of a tax was of far less importance than its administrative serviceability. Now the position is reversed, and an equitable basis is the overriding consideration. Administration must accommodate itself to the needs of equity even at the expense of greater cost and loss of economy in levy.

4. Rates do in fact provide an equitable general basis on which to raise local revenues, and, in so far as they fall short of the highest standards of equity in the light of modern thought, they have been shown to be capable of modification and reform. They have one attribute of incalculable value. They are founded on principle and not on any arbitrary basis. That principle is that the annual value or letting value of the property the ratepayer occupies represents a true measure of what he should pay. Exceptions and modifications of this rule where its operation cuts across current sociological and fiscal principles are of very limited extent. That is in contradistinction, e.g. to income tax, for which even the ascertainment of income is subject to a mass of arbitrary rules and the allowances made and the graded rates of charge are purely arbitrary.

Validity of Annual Value Basis

5. This annual value basis derives its validity from six factors related to the local government services provided and the parties benefiting from them:

(1) It represents a tax on accommodation to defray the cost of services for that accommodation.

(2) Accommodation benefits from those services.

(3) The provision and use of that accommodation involves an increase direct or indirect in the cost of those services.

(4) The cost is logically apportioned among the separate occupiers of the accommodation in proportion each to the value of his accommodation—what it is worth his while to pay for it, i.e. its rent or annual value.

(5) Part of the total annual value of property is attributable to the services— without them the accommodation would have no value.

(6) The rate is a tax on expenditure which the ratepayer elects to incur and its level in any particular case is determined by what property the ratepayer decides to occupy.

6. Rates are a tax on accommodation fundamentally because they provide services for the accommodation and its occupants. They are not properly a charge for local services, but a levy raised to defray their cost. That is the justification for charging them on the accommodation and its occupants. Nevertheless the services are of several classes and some of them have a dual character. Many of them are services also to residents in the district irrespective of their occupation of accommodation, and many to outsiders merely visiting or passing through the locality or to the community as a whole. The classes are as follows:—

(a) Those which are purely services to accommodation, such as sewerage and drainage generally, public health covering sanitation, cleansing, refuse disposal, etc., the fire service and town planning.

(b) Those which are basically concerned with accommodation though rather as a locality than as individual units, but which are enjoyed by individuals; these include the provision of amenities such as parks, recreation grounds, baths, washhouses, public libraries and street lighting. Both these classes of function can be treated as rendered wholly to accommodation and therefore can logically have the charge for them based on the value of the accommodation. These services are not restricted by the amount of accommodation enjoyed.

(c) Services which are of a dual character, since they serve both accommodation and individuals such as highways and bridges (making, improvement, maintenance, and cleansing), police, housing and education. Highways naturally serve premises, but they cater equally for general traffic of individuals irrespective of residence in the area. Police are in a parallel position since they safeguard property but equally protect individuals whoever and wherever they are in the locality. Housing serves accommodation indirectly only, though it serves the locality as a whole. But it is to a great extent also a service to individuals, a social service and a national service, so is education, although it is naturally an invaluable amenity for accommodation. While some part of the cost of this class (in varying proportions) is therefore logically apportioned on the value of the accommodation benefited, the remainder is more naturally charged on ability to pay through national taxation.

(d) Health services under the National Health Service Act, and provision for the aged, infirm and handicapped. These are properly a social and national service, for the benefit of individuals as distinct from accommodation. The value of the accommodation is therefore irrelevant as a form of taxation and some other form such as ability to pay would be more appropriate.

7. A considerable part of local expenditure is today properly financed on the value of local accommodation (rates); another considerable part (including education which in cost may be equal to all the rest put together), is more appropriately financed partly on the value of accommodation (rates) and partly on ability to pay (income tax); and a small part is more equitably financed on ability to pay (income tax). This approach is fully recognised in the financing of local government today, grants from the Exchequer representing taxation on ability to pay somewhat exceeding the yield of rates.

8. All classes of lands and heritages benefit from the services provided by local authorities as a typical selection shows:

(1) Dwelling houses clearly benefit from all of the first three classes.

(2) Business premises such as shops, offices, licensed premises, theatres and cinemas, garages and warehouses, all benefit from class (a) e.g., drainage, refuse collection, fire service and town planning. They benefit indirectly from the amenity facilities, in that anything which improves the locality attracts people and enhances the local business potential. As profit-earning premises, in any event, however, there is good ground for charging them on their values as accommodation for the benefit accorded to the customers who make their livelihood. They benefit indirectly also from housing (providing customers) and education but fully from highways, and police.

(3) Factories and industrial premises are in a similar position but are more directly benefited by the amenity facilities and housing and education, which are necessary for contented workers.

(4) Clubs and sports grounds benefit directly from class (a) functions, and highways, police and housing, and to some extent from amenity facilities and education.

9. Thus class (a) services benefit fully all classes of heritages, class (b) all (but some to a less extent) and class (c) mainly all (again some to a less extent).

10. Practically all forms of accommodation involve directly or indirectly the cost of local government functions. A single heritage, as the unit of accommodation is called, may make no appreciable difference, but the accumulation of heritages, the sum total of accommodation, is the basic cause of the whole of local expenditure, for without the accommodation that expenditure would not exist.

11. The ordinary classes of rateable heritage illustrate this. Houses, business premises, (shops, offices, licensed premises, theatres and cinemas and garages) warehouses, factories and other industrial premises, and clubs and sports grounds all increase the strain on the class (a) services such as drainage, refuse collection and the fire service. Houses also add to the cost of class (b) services (local amenities). Business premises do not add directly to the cost of amenity facilities, or of housing and education, but they do to that of highways and police. Factories add directly or indirectly (and heavily) to the cost of all services. Clubs and sports grounds do not increase the cost of class (b) functions or of housing and education but they do of highways and police.

12. There is solid ground therefore for all classes of accommodation to contribute to all classes of local expenditure (except class d). It is reasonable also to make the contribution a pre-emptive charge based, e.g. on the value of the accommodation to its occupier, and made irrespective of whether the occupation shows a profit or a loss and irrespective of what any profit may be.

13. The fact that rates are a charge on accommodation itself imports largely that the charge should be related to the value of the accommodation. The charge is made on the occupier of the accommodation. It should therefore presumably be based on the value of the accommodation to the occupier. That means the rental value or annual value.

14. In Scotland this value, in the case of dwelling-houses, is not the rental value in the open market, but the hypothetical rent at which the dwelling-houses might reasonably be expected to let from year to year. This means that the assessments on which rates are based are not so closely related to each other as might be desirable and do not properly reflect the differences in value between dwelling-houses and other subjects. This anomaly could be removed. The proper relation of assessments to true values and to each other would then be established and where fully achieved it would import the correct assessment of all the ratepayers concerned absolutely and in relation to each other.

15. The basis of annual value is reinforced by the fact that there are two constituent elements of that annual value in rateable heritages. One of these is the physical heritage itself. The other is the locality in which it is situated, with all its building and other development and, above all, its local services. Take away the heritage itself and the value will be negligible. Take away all the physical aspects of the rest of the locality, and particularly the local services, and again the heritage will be of little value. There remains the fact that the local services also contribute to the value of the rateable heritage itself in maintaining the rental value of the heritage.

16. It is thus logical to treat part of the rental value of the heritage as being in respect of the services. The obvious corollary is that part of the rent obtainable for the heritage should be applied to the provision of those services. That is precisely what happens in rating. The total rental value of the heritage is actually its ordinary rental value plus the rates charged on it. The charging of rates is simply an appropriation of part of the rental value to the cost of the services maintaining it.

17. This is a well recognised principle of rating law. It means, of course, that any abrogation of the rating system would be followed by a general increase in rents, and so appropriate to landlords the rental value previously appropriated to local services.

18. The annual value basis is the natural one from the ratepayer's point of view. This is because rates are a tax on expenditure as distinct from a tax on income. That means that liability arises only if the ratepayer elects to incur the expenditure—if he chooses to occupy property. A person who is able to effect his purpose without occupying property does not pay rates except indirectly. That he can do by being a lodger instead of a householder, an itinerant showman instead of a hall proprietor, a mobile caravan owner instead of one on a permanent site, the inhabitant of a yacht instead of the occupant of a boathouse, an employee instead of a shopkeeper or businessman in an office, the hirer of rooms or playing fields for recreation instead of the occupier of a club or sports ground and so on.

19. More important (because the vast majority of ratepayers must occupy property just as they must eat food) is that the ratepayer can determine where he is going to incur his liability to pay rates and how much (or at least proportionately how much) he is going to pay. Thus he knows what kind of property he wants (house, shop, office, etc.),,he knows what outlay he can afford, whether in the form of rent or of equivalent lost interest on the capital outlay by way of purchase. Then, as rates are geared to the rental value of the heritage he chooses, he automatically decides what rates he can afford at the same time, and elects to pay them.

20. In the ordinary way, therefore, the ratepayer cannot complain that his rates are excessive (provided the value is right), because he has himself chosen to pay them. But this can apply only if rates are based on the annual value of the property, because only then will they be what the ratepayer has decided he can afford to pay. If there is any departure from this basis, any distortion of value, e.g. through another basis of value, this great advantage of the rating system is lost, and the personal circumstances of the ratepayer come into the account.

21. One important qualification of this principle applies to residential accommodation, for two reasons. One is that houses are in short supply and many ratepayers are therefore driven to take accommodation which is really beyond what they can afford. The other is that there is a level of accommodation and of rent below which it is impossible to find premises and that even this standard is beyond the means of the low income ratepayer. These two injustices are now broadly removed by the rate rebate scheme under the Rating Act, 1966.

22. The conclusion to be drawn from the foregoing would seem to be inescapably that rental value is the natural and logical basis of charge for class (*a*) and class (*b*) services and for a considerable part of class (*c*) services.

Advantages of the Rating System

23. It is the foundation on which local government rests today, providing a means of raising revenue which can be left completely in the hands of local authorities with virtually no Government control and the minimum of legal rules restricting their freedom of action. Taking rates away, without providing an equally satisfactory alternative, means destroying the main prop of independent local government and with it the essence of local government itself as understood in Britain today.

24. It is simple to understand. Large numbers of ratepayers conduct their own appeals with full understanding of what is involved, and those who do not grasp the basis are mainly those who would not understand that of any tax at all.

25. The primary difficulties of assessment have been resolved over the years by the evolution of valuation techniques and by legislative provisions.

26. Exemptions and reliefs (inevitable in any system of taxation) have been largely rationalised in recent years. One outstanding anomaly is the exemption of agricultural land and agricultural buildings, which have not been valued since 1956.

27. The system is extremely simple to operate (although complications have resulted from the recently introduced rebate and instalment systems—inevitable results of reforms to mitigate hardship). There is no annual revaluation. Valuations are already in the valuation roll and are carried into the assessment roll and used for the preparation of demand notes as soon as the rate in the £ is determined.

28. The process of collection and recovery is well defined, simple and effective. Rates are a universally recognised liability and they are paid reasonably promptly in the vast majority of cases. The fringe of slow payers can normally be brought to pay in due course by the straightforward recovery proceedings.

29. Cost of collection (the expense incurred in collecting rates) is very low. Loss on collection (the items written off as irrecoverable) is also very low. Rates rank in this respect as one of the most economical (and economic) of taxes.

30. The yield—about £1,500 million a year in the United Kingdom—is impressive and represents nearly half the total local authority revenue (including grants but excluding trading and other special revenue).

31. The yield is certain and predictable. A rating authority can make a rate knowing that the ultimate rate product will be very close to its estimate (exceptions are comparatively few). Balances for contingencies can therefore be kept at a low level.

Criticisms of the Rating System

32. Rates have been severely criticised in recent years, and it is as well to understand the basis of the criticisms and how far they are justifiable.

33. Any form of tax is unpopular with those who have to pay it, and rates have a widespread incidence. The consequence is that any criticism of rating finds a ready echo among all sections of the community, and, whether sound or unsound, is taken up and repeated as further evidence of the inequity (or more appropriately in the ratepayer's view iniquity) of the rating system. Many people feel the same about income tax, but those who suffer from it most are too few in number to make its inequities (or iniquities?) generally felt.

34. Rates produce a very large revenue. Income tax is a much heavier burden, but its weight with the mass of the population and particularly the lower income groups is comparatively much less owing to the steep grading of incidence. The result is that rates are more severely felt and more generally disliked.

35. Persistent inflation and ever-rising costs add relentlessly to the cost of local services. Those services also grow faster than the national income. The result is a yearly rise in the rate burden reflected in appreciable proportionate all round increases every year in the rates demanded from practically every ratepayer, and increases moreover out of proportion to the rises in incomes and prices. This causes extreme resentment.

36. The annual values of rateable property on which rates are based are revised every five years at the quinquennial revaluations. The new values necessarily reflect the effects of five years of inflation and show mainly considerable increases. But they also show large differences in the amounts of the increases for different properties, some being doubled, some increased by varying percentages and a few even reduced. The resulting reduction in rate poundage leaves many paying about the same, many paying more and some paying less.

37. Houses are under-valued in terms of current value (but correctly in terms of the Valuation and Rating (Scotland) Act, 1956) while shops are valued on a current value basis under the same Act. This had led to litigation which has been given publicity and has caused misunderstanding of the system.

38. None of these causes of unpopularity of the rating system constitutes a major defect. Any alternative method of taxation will be equally unpopular—with those who have to pay it. It will be just as heavy because the same amount would have to be raised for local government purposes—possibly heavier if the aim were to transfer part of the cost borne by Government grants to local taxation. Unless local spending is checked, it too will have to increase annually. The Prices and Incomes policy could make a major contribution, if successful.

39. The rate incidence problem would be further aggravated if quinquennial revaluations are not strictly adhered to and if current valuation rolls are not constantly brought up to date whenever changes in value occur. The irregularities in incidence, although not yet experienced in Scotland, have occurred in England due to the transfer of the function of valuation for rating to the Inland Revenue Valuation Office resulting in delay and abandonment of quinquennial revaluations.

40. The Inland Revenue Valuation Office in England was placed in the position of having to confess its inability to do work for which it is responsible. A major cause must rest with failure to provide conditions of service which will tempt new entrants into it— a failure to realise the great importance of the work. A second equally important factor is the postponement of valuation for rating purposes (involving ratepayers in taxation of over £1,000m. a year) to other purposes such as valuation under the Land Commission Bill, which will involve only fractions of that sum. The present position raises very seriously the question of whether the "nationalisation" of valuation in England in 1948–50 is a failure, and whether, if larger local government units are to come, the process of valuation should be entrusted to the larger authorities newly constituted.

41. Besides these matters, there are four major criticisms of the rating system which have to be considered. Rather curiously these are much less the cause of the unpopularity of rates than the factors already given.

42. It is said that rate revenue does not expand to keep pace with the national income and that this is the basic cause of annual increases of rate poundages, imposing a proportionate increase on all ratepayers instead of particular increases on those who have shared in the growth of the national income. This is a mis-statement of the true position. More than half the annual rate increases can be attributed to increases of local expenditure disproportionate to the growth of the national income already referred to. They would therefore fall to be raised in this way with any form of taxation.

43. The remainder is attributable to the time-lag implicit in quinquennial revaluations. Annual values rise to keep pace with the general price level, but the rise is only reflected in valuation rolls at quinquennial revaluations. In the intervening period part of the balance of increased expenditure is in fact met by increases of total values from new and altered properties and redevelopment. The remainder and inflation of costs are provided for by higher rate poundages, i.e. proportionately for everybody. For the first two years this is largely immaterial. Variations in appreciation of value may become more noticeable on the third and succeeding years, but proportionate increases are not a serious distortion of liability.

44. The reference to being proportionate to increased income (not always advanced) is irrelevant, because it means importing into rates pure ability to pay as distinguished from ability to pay as reflected in annual value.

45. Rates are criticised as not being based on ability to pay. Criticism framed in this way is made only by those for whom "ability to pay" is the be-all and end-all of every form of taxation, and its overriding essential. It ignores the principle of holding the balance of taxation between income and expenditure. Income tax is a tax on income, which is appropriate for national taxation, where questions of location of income are minimal and uniformity over the whole country is secured. It would be inappropriate to duplicate it with a competing tax at local level, where difficulties of location of income and of wide variations of rates over the country are almost insuperable. They are matched by the serious danger of the whole of a man's income (and more) being swallowed by the double tax. Moreover, it is hardly credible that, e.g. a millionaire deriving little advantage from local services should be the mainstay of a locality, as he might be on the basis of local income tax. Such a position could have cataclysmic consequences from the taxpayer's removal elsewhere.

46. Rates are a tax on expenditure and as such are complementary to income tax. As a tax on expenditure, as already shown, their incidence is determined within limits by the ratepayer himself. He selects the property for which he is rated, and he selects it in the light of what he can afford. This is admittedly strictly within limits owing to the general shortage of accommodation. But the position is radically different from that of income tax, where liability is inescapable.

47. Rates are said to be contrary to modern principles of taxation because they are regressive, the liability of the lower income groups being proportionately much higher than that of the higher levels of income. This is a valid criticism, though as rates are complementary to income tax, their joint effects should be looked at rather than rates in isolation. However, the regressive nature of rates, which of course affects only residential accommodation, has been largely provided for by the system of rate rebates instituted by the Rating Act, 1966, an ingenious piece of legislation, experience of which will probably lead to important improvements in the future.

48. It is noteworthy that a Government which has made great play with the regressive nature of rates has not scrupled to introduce a national tax, which is far more regressive and a tax on labour and it is charged equally on the £10 and £100 a week employee—and on the £20,000 a year executive (though of course the employer pays).

49. In the sense of being directly liable, it is true that many people who enjoy the full benefit of local services never pay rates at all. This is because only the occupier is rateable, so that any co-residents such as his wife, grown-up children, boarders, etc., pay nothing to the rating authority. The consequence is that a single person, a married couple, a large family, and even two or three families may occupy similar houses and be charged each only one lot of rates, the same amount throughout. This is an extreme case, and it may indicate that some amendment of rating law analogous to the rebate system is desirable to meet it, though like the vacant property rate it may be unproductive of much income. In the vast majority of cases liability is reasonably related to user.

50. However, it is wrong to suppose that people who do not pay rates directly do not pay them in fact at all. It is common knowledge that the contributions of grown-up children to the family budget take into account the rate liability. Boarders and lodgers and residents in guest houses and hotels all pay charges which take the rate liability of the premises into account, though they probably pay less in rates than direct ratepayers. It may be as indicated, that either a modification of rating law or less a supplementary residents' tax (based on or limited by annual value) is called for.

51. The foregoing analysis shows that there is nothing fundamentally bad in the rating system, though there are certainly aspects which could do with scrutiny with a view to some reform.

52. Its importance as an essential part of a national taxation policy and its particular usefulness in ensuring a fair distribution of the cost of local government services will no doubt be borne in mind when the financial aspects of local government reform are considered.

Memorandum by the
Association of Lands Valuation Assessors of Scotland

1. The Association of Lands Valuation Assessors of Scotland thanks the Royal Commission for the opportunity to submit evidence relating to its terms of reference.

2. The Association was originally constituted in 1886. As a consequence of the Valuation and Rating (Scotland) Act 1956 it was reconstituted in 1957 and now consists of all twenty-three Assessors appointed under that Act and, as associate members, seventeen Depute Assessors. All members are Fellows or Professional Associates of the Royal Institution of Chartered Surveyors and are solely responsible in their own areas for the valuation of lands and heritages as defined in the Valuation Acts. All Assessors also hold appointments as Electoral Registration Officers in their respective areas. The objects of the Association are to encourage amongst members the exchange of ideas regarding their statutory duties and to promote uniformity in operating the provisions of the Valuation Acts and the Representation of the People Acts.

3. While in the remit to the Royal Commission there was no specific mention of local government finance, the Association is of the opinion that a viable system of local democracy cannot be sustained unless there are available to local authorities independent sources of income within their own control and sufficient to meet a substantial proportion of their expenditure. Accordingly, it is felt that local finance must inevitably be considered by the Royal Commission.

4. The Members of the Association believe that as Lands Valuation Assessors they are in a position to make comments and suggestions on methods of financing local government and the major part of this memorandum is concerned with this subject. Certain other matters within the terms of reference of the Royal Commission are also considered. The memorandum can conveniently be presented under the following headings:

(1) A review of the existing system of financing local government services, and observations on some suggested alternative systems.

(2) Consideration of methods whereby the present system might be altered to make it more effective and to widen the base of local revenue.

(3) Comments on areas and functions.

A REVIEW OF THE EXISTING SYSTEM OF FINANCING LOCAL GOVERNMENT SERVICES, AND OBSERVATIONS ON SOME SUGGESTED ALTERNATIVE SYSTEMS

5. In 1954 the Scottish Valuation and Rating Committee (the Sorn Committee) issued their Report (Cmd. 9244), having enquired into "the system by which funds are raised locally to defray the expenses of local government and by which the liability of individual persons to contribute to such funds is determined".

6. The Committee came to the conclusion that neither a local income tax, taxation of site values nor a local poll tax is practicable and, provided it is not overloaded, the existing system of levying rates on heritable property should be continued subject to suggested modifications. They recommended *inter alia* that valuations should be dissociated from actual rents and should be related to "fair" rent on current values, and that all properties should be revalued every five years.

7. These recommendations were incorporated in the Valuation and Rating (Scotland) Act, 1956 and in the Association's experience the results have proved satisfactory. In particular the "fair" rent provisions do result in a substantial degree of equity among

ratepayers. On the other hand the tax base of local authorities is steadily being eroded by the exclusion from valuation of certain categories of subject, by the restrictions placed on the valuations of others, and by the granting of rating relief to certain types of property. Comments and suggestions are made at a later stage in this memorandum.

8. In the opinion of the Association the necessary independent source of income referred to earlier in this memorandum is already available in the proceeds derived from rates.

Criticisms of the Present Rating System

9. In recent years, the rating system has come under criticism because it is said to be (*a*) narrowly based, (*b*) "regressive", (*c*) insufficiently buoyant, (*d*) a deterrent to improvement of property and (*e*) in no way related to ability to pay. It might be appropriate at this point to consider these criticisms.

Narrow base of taxation

10. Narrowness of base implies that not enough people contribute and because of omissions from valuation and the effect of derating this is probably true, but later in this memorandum a solution is offered.

Rating is a regressive tax

11. Rating is a far less regressive tax than any other expenditure tax. This was clearly shown in Table 59, page 22, of the Report by the Committee of Inquiry into the impact of rates on Households, Cmnd. 2582 (The Allen Report). On examining this Table it is interesting to note that whereas when rates are expressed as a percentage of income, the percentage falls as income increases, the actual *amount* paid increases as income increases. It is also of note that the amount paid tends to fall as the number of dependents increases.

Rating is not a buoyant tax

12. In 1961/62, the total rateable value of Scotland was £99 million. During the inter-revaluation years the total rose by about 2% every year reaching £108 million in 1965/66. The estimated rateable value in 1966/67 is £139 million which shows an increase over the quinquennium of 7% per annum which is a higher annual rate than the growth in the national economy in recent years. This criticism probably arises from the very high rate of growth in local authority expenditure which far exceeds the growth in the national economy.

A deterrent to improvement of property

13. There may be a few instances where an owner has decided against improving or developing his property because of the possible rating consequences, but in the experience of the Association there is no body of evidence that the system has acted as a deterrent to the improvement and development of property in general. It is considered that the high capital cost of building is the main deterrent. It might be observed here that this criticism emerges mainly in connection with proposals to make small additions or improvements to existing houses: the initial erection of a house is itself an "improvement" to the land on which it is built, but the initial valuation is not criticised as a tax on "improvements".

In no way related to ability to pay

14. This criticism arises from a natural inclination to compare rates with the principal personal tax, namely Income Tax. As already mentioned, the amount of rates paid by residential ratepayers generally increases as the average income increases. Within this broad trend, however, there are many whose liability for rates exceeds their ability to pay. The Rating Act 1966 now provides for a rebate of rates on dwelling houses based on the

income of the occupier. Relief is also given to charitable organisations in terms of the Local Government (Financial Provisions etc.) (Scotland) Act 1962. Such provisions have met to a substantial degree the criticism under this head. So far as industry and commerce are concerned firms usually occupy premises suited to their business and therefore to their ability to pay.

Alternative Sources of Revenue

15. Before considering the advantages of the present rating system it is thought appropriate to refer to alternative and supplementary systems of financing local government which have been suggested from time to time.

Local Income Tax

16. Local income tax has been proposed as an alternative or as a supplement to local rates but has seldom been precisely defined. It has been suggested as an addition to the standard rate of national Income Tax, the proceeds of which would be remitted by the Exchequer to the local authorities according to a formula. This is precisely the system by which Exchequer grant is presently distributed to local authorities and if adopted would not provide the independent source of income deemed necessary to sustain a viable system of local democracy.

17. A variation of the above suggestion is that local authorities should be allocated a specific proportion of all national revenue. Apart from the conflict which might very well arise between national and local government interests over the level of taxation at any particular time, there would be obvious difficulties in determining the apportionment of the total revenue between national and local government, and among the various local authorities. The primary objection would again be the lack of an independent source of income and of control by the authority.

18. Before a Local Income Tax could be justified the local authority must have the power to determine the rate of tax and to receive as a right the revenue so raised. Only two possible approaches would satisfy these conditions; firstly by each local authority being responsible for fixing, assessing, levying and collecting the tax, and secondly by the rate of Local Income Tax being fixed by the individual authority and thereafter assessed, levied and collected by the Inland Revenue with the national Income Tax. The Association is unable to envisage practicable or reasonable administrative arrangements to provide for the first approach.

19. The inherent difficulties and disadvantages in the second approach could only be overcome after a major reorganisation of local government administration, and even then it is doubtful if such a system would provide a fair basis of local taxation.

Rating of Site Values

20. In recent years a number of individuals and organisations have advocated the rating or taxing of site values, being a tax levied on the owner and based on the unimproved value (i.e. bare site value) of all land. It is generally suggested that such a tax would encourage development and redevelopment and that the burden of the tax could not be passed on to the occupier. It is also suggested that the proceeds of such a tax would be recovered by the local authorities from whose actions much of the increase in the land values arises.

21. The proceeds of a tax on site values might well provide a supplement to local authority income but the system of site value rating as a whole would not in the Association's view provide a reasonable alternative to the present rating system. It would share to some extent the merits and demerits of the present rating system, but with a narrower base. The main objection to it, however, arises from the inherent difficulties of valuation.

There is little direct evidence on which to base site values. It may be, however, that rating of site values is no longer a practical possibility in view of the Government's current proposals for a Land Commission and the levying of a tax on the development value of land. This opinion is supported by the conclusions of a Working Party formed by the Royal Institution of Chartered Surveyors in November 1964 to consider and report on this subject.

Rating on Capital Value

22. It has been suggested that annual value is no longer a reliable basis on which to charge local taxation and that there would be advantages in using capital value. It is envisaged that such values would be prepared on the basis of the existing use of the property (i.e. ignoring the value of any potential change of use which would require planning permission).

23. A system based on these considerations would undoubtedly produce considerable changes in the incidence of rating between one class of property and another. The primary objection to this system, however, is that capital value is the value to the owner whereas rates are normally considered as a charge on occupation.

24. On a superficial consideration of the relative merits of using capital and rental evidence in arriving at value it might be considered that sale prices would provide a more substantial and reliable body of evidence than rentals. This has not proved to be so. Irrelevant considerations can affect individual sale prices to such an extent that they would not provide a reliable guide in arriving at a uniform basis of valuation. Evidence of rentals, although less numerous than sales in some classes of property, provide a more consistent and reliable basis. The interpretation of rental evidence has provided no difficulty to Assessors in the past and it is not anticipated that it would do so in the future.

25. Despite these criticisms it is considered that of all the possible alternatives to rental value capital valuation is the only one which could provide a satisfactory basis for the financing of local government. Nevertheless, to derive a reliable and uniform basis from capital values would be difficult and this basis would not in the long run be more satisfactory than the existing system.

Supplementary Sources of Income

Motor Vehicle Duty

26. It has been suggested that local authorities should be allocated either all or part of a specific national revenue. Motor vehicle duty has been mentioned in this connection. The Association consider that this suggestion has merit, especially as the duty is collected locally. If the whole revenue was received by local authorities it would meet about 9% of the total local expenditure. At present the tax is levied at uniform national rates but it might be feasible that local authorities could be permitted to vary the rates either as they wished or within a prescribed range. This, of course, would only be practicable if the whole revenue was received by local authorities.

27. Other national taxes which might be wholly or partially allocated to local authorities are Purchase Tax and Excise Tax on gaming machines and gambling establishments.

Poll Tax

28. A possible supplementary source of local revenue would be a simple Poll Tax levied at a rate per head on all electors who are not ratepayers. This tax would be relatively simple to administer but would require to be based on the Register of Electors. It was concluded in the Sorn Report (para. 7, page 7) that "There are objections in principle to associating registration as a voter with liability to tax". A further criticism is that a Poll Tax is regressive.

Residence Tax

29. A variation of a Poll Tax has recently been suggested whereby each adult over 21 years of age normally resident in a dwelling house, with the exception of the spouse of the householder, would be assessed for rates as if he were the sole occupier of the house. This tax would also require to be based on the Register of Electors and would be open to the same criticisms as a Poll Tax.

Sales Tax

30. Another supplementary method of raising local revenue sometimes suggested is by way of a Sales Tax, presumably taking the form of a locally fixed percentage added to the retail price of all goods and services. The levy of such a tax on essential goods and services would be regressive; the administrative difficulties in levying and collecting would be enormous, and the tax would conflict with the operation of the national Purchase Tax which is well established and effective and therefore unlikely to be withdrawn. In these circumstances it is unlikely that a Sales Tax would prove acceptable to either the taxpayer or the Government.

Advantages of the present rating system

31. Having reviewed the criticisms of, and the alternatives to the present system its advantages can now be considered.

32. By contrast to national Income Tax, which is levied solely on the basis of ability to pay, the present rating system ensures that contributions towards the cost of providing local services are made by all households. It has been established that on average this contribution by domestic occupiers increases as income increases. In Scotland, the rateable values of domestic subjects in 1965/66 represented 52% of the total rateable value and, after allowing for the contribution by way of Government Grant, the rates levied on domestic subjects represented 22.8% of the total net cost of the rate fund services. It is apparent therefore that householders meet directly by rates less than one quarter of the net cost of local authority services.

33. The system is reasonably productive and flexible, and its yield is easy to calculate.

34. The cost of administration and collection is low, being less as a percentage of rate revenue than is the cost of collection of Income Tax as a percentage of gross receipts. It is also simple to collect.

35. It is virtually impossible to avoid payment of rates as they are based on immovable property. The scope for "tax avoidance" in local rating it extremely limited.

36. It might be claimed that the rating system creates an incentive for persons to move to accommodation which is more suitable to their needs and therefore to their ability to pay rather than to occupy excess accommodation.

37. It would appear that the majority of ratepayers appreciate the simple principle that rates are paid by the occupier of the property on an estimated rental value.

38. The recent introduction of rate rebates and payment by instalments has to a great extent eliminated a major source of criticism so far as domestic ratepayers are concerned.

39. In deciding the merits of a form of taxation the advantages and disadvantages cannot be considered in isolation from all other forms of taxation. What might in isolation be considered to be a defect may turn out to have compensating features when considered in the whole system of taxation. This is considered to be the case with the rating system. The very fact that it is "regressive" offsets to an extent the very "progressive" nature of income tax and ensures that all households who benefit from the essentially local and personal services provided by local authorities contribute to some extent towards the cost.

40. The present system of local taxation in this country accords with the systems operated in many other countries in that it is based on real property. Other local taxes in these countries are usually of a supplementary nature.

41. Various committees and working parties have considered in recent years the means by which the rating system might be replaced by alternative forms of revenue. Invariably it has been decided that the difficulties inherent in these alternative systems have been so great as to preclude their introduction, and that the present system should be retained subject to improvement where possible.

SUGGESTED IMPROVEMENTS TO THE PRESENT SYSTEM

42. Having advanced reasons for the belief that the present form of local rating on heritable property should continue, the Association now wishes to draw the attention of the Royal Commission to what are believed to be certain shortcomings in the operation of the present law. The improvements suggested are directed towards broadening the base of local taxation, rendering it more buoyant and more acceptable to the majority of ratepayers.

43. The principal direction regarding the scope of the Valuation Roll is contained in Section 1 of the Lands Valuation (Scotland) Act, 1854, which directs that "the whole lands and heritages" within the county or burgh shall be entered in the Roll. Subsequent legislation has made exceptions to this general rule.

44. In practice, the operation of the exempting provisions of this subsequent legislation has caused anomalies, and inequity in the distribution of the rate burden has resulted. Since 1854 there has been a tendency on the one hand to make exemptions from entry in the Roll of certain properties, and on the other hand to modify the principle of uniformity of valuation by allowing figures other than those representing fair rental value to be entered.

45. The anomalies caused by the latter development will be dealt with in a later section of this Memorandum. Consideration is now given to those resulting from the former.

Subjects excluded from Valuation

Agricultural land and buildings

46. The favourable rating treatment of agricultural subjects was introduced in 1896 by the Agricultural Rates (Scotland) Act, which provided for the remission of five-eighths of the occupiers' rates payable on agricultural subjects. It was continued and extended by the Rating and Valuation (Scotland) Act of 1929, Section 44 of which provided for a deduction of eighty-seven and one-half per cent from the gross annual value to arrive at rateable value. The present position is regulated by Section 7 of the Valuation and Rating (Scotland) Act, 1956, which provides for the complete exclusion from the Valuation Roll of agricultural land and buildings. Agricultural dwelling-houses are, however, entered in the Roll.

Net salmon fishings

47. Section 7(2) of the Local Government and Financial Provisions (Scotland) Act 1958, provides for the exclusion from the Valuation Roll of net salmon fishings. Dwelling-houses, bothies etc. associated with net fishings are, however, entered in the Roll.

Railways and railway subjects and subjects occupied by an Electricity Board

48. The Local Government Act of 1948 provides that no premises which are, or form part of, railway or canal lands and heritages, or lands and heritages occupied by an Electricity Board shall be entered in the Valuation Roll, and no rates shall be levied in respect of these properties. This provision, however, does not exempt from valuation and entry in the Roll all subjects forming part of these Undertakings; for example, a dwelling-house, hotel or refreshment rooms, premises so let out as to be capable of separate assessment, or property concerned with road transport, sea transport, or harbours, are excluded from the exempting provisions. For the present purpose (which is to indicate an undesirable trend of development) it is not thought necessary to go into details at this stage. The effect of the exempting provisions is that a substantial number of lands and heritages, of considerable and increasing value, are excluded from entry in valuation rolls throughout the country.

49. This does not mean, of course, that no contribution is made to local authorities to meet the loss of rates. The Act provides that the British Transport Authority and Electricity Boards shall, in the year 1948–49 and in subsequent years, make payments to the Secretary of State for Scotland in lieu of rates, according to a formula set forth in the Act. This formula is based on the rates paid according to the valuations which were fixed in the year 1947–48, varied according to certain stated circumstances affecting these undertakings. The payments so made are allocated to rating authorities according to the rateable values of their areas, and are not related to the value of property actually occupied by the statutory undertakers within a local authority area.

Parks

50. Section 19 of the Local Government (Financial Provisions) (Scotland) Act 1963 excludes from entry in the Roll any lands and heritages consisting of a park vested in, or under the control of, a local authority, and from which the local authority does not derive profit. This provision has been judicially held to apply to golf courses owned or administered by a local authority, and applies also to tennis courts. bowling greens, etc. under the control of local authorities.

Sewers etc.

51. Section 8 of the Valuation and Rating (Scotland) Act, 1956 excludes from entry in the Roll a number of categories of subject, of which the most important, from the point of view of numbers and potential rateable value is sewers.

Observations on subjects excluded from Valuation

52. The exclusion from the Valuation Roll of these several properties is a departure from the original intention that all lands and heritages should be represented in the roll, and has brought about a loss of rates and a consequent shift in the rating burden. The effect has been to narrow the base of local rating.

53. It is suggested that the circumstances in which agricultural land and buildings were first partially derated and, more recently, exempted altogether from rating no longer prevail. It is considered that there is a strong case for the complete re-rating of these subjects. If, however, the Commission is unable to support full re-rating of agricultural land, it is strongly urged that re-rating of agricultural buildings at least be considered. As the law now stands most agricultural buildings are excluded from the roll but certain buildings, mainly those used for the intensive feeding of livestock, are not. (See the recent decision by the Lands Valuation Appeal Court in the case of Peddie *v.* Assessor for Roxburgh 1964).

WE 12—G

54. It has not proved possible to ascertain any sufficient reason for the exclusion from the roll of net salmon fishings.

55. It is suggested that the provisions of the Local Government Act, 1948, whereby railway and electricity subjects are excluded from the roll, subject to a formula-based payment in lieu of rates should be repealed and the undertakings should be come subject to valuation and local rating.

56. The exclusion from the roll of public parks by virtue of Section 19 of the Local Government (Financial Provisions) (Scotland) Act, 1963, has had the effect of creating anomalies in excluding local authority owned golf courses, (including those at St. Andrews), bowling greens, tennis courts, and playing-fields from the roll, but not privately-owned subjects of the same kind.

57. The exclusion of sewers may stem from a reluctance to inflate the rates by merely transferring payments from one public pocket to another, but seems illogical so long as telephone wires, water-pipes etc. are included in the roll.

58. In order to remove anomalies and in the interests of a more uniform distribution of the rate burden. it is for consideration whether those exempted properties, or some of them, should be made the subject of normal valuation and rating. While it is recognised that the omission of certain properties from valuation may be necessary in exceptional cases, the policy of granting relief from rates in this manner, if carried too far creates a situation where the exemptions have a prejudicial effect on the general principle. Perhaps it is not too much to say that this method of affording relief from rates is somewhat in the nature of a subsidy to the favoured ratepayer and that it is preferable from many points of view that a subsidy or relief from rates should be openly awarded rather than that the burden of rates should itself be modified or concealed.

Subjects whose annual value is restricted

59. A notable development in the law of valuation is the extent to which the principle of uniformity of valuation, referred to in the preamble to the 1854 Act, has been interfered with by later legislation. The preamble states—"Whereas it is expedient that *one uniform valuation* be established of lands and heritages in Scotland according to which all public assessments leviable or that may be levied according to the real rent of such lands and heritages may be assessed and collected, and that provision be made for such valuation being annually revised".

60. There has been a tendency to modify this principle of uniformity of valuation by allowing figures other than those representing fair rental value to be entered in the roll. Consideration is now given to the anomalies resulting from these.

Dwelling-houses

61. It is considered that the present statutory provisions relating to the valuation of dwelling-houses are unsatisfactory. In terms of Section 6(2) of the Valuation and Rating (Scotland) Act, 1956, the gross annual value of any dwelling-house is "the rent at which the [house] might reasonably be expected to let from year to year". Difficulties have been caused by the direction contained in Section 6(4) of the Act, which is in the following terms:

"In ascertaining under subsection (2) of this section the gross annual value of any dwelling-house—

"(*a*) it shall be assumed that at the material time all the comparable accommodation in the locality is due shortly to become available for letting free from any restrictions (whether on rent or on recovery of possession) imposed by or under any enactment and rents to be fixed without regard to any contributions payable by the Secretary of State or the local authority in respect of local authority houses or houses provided by a housing association or a development corporation and without regard to the terms on which structures are made available to a local authority under section one of the Housing (Temporary Accommodation) Act, 1944, and that no marked deficiency or excess exists in the amount of such accommodation as compared with the number of persons acceptable as tenants of such accommodation and genuinely competing for tenancies thereof;

(*b*) no account shall be taken of any statutory provision restricting the classes of person to whom the lands and heritages may be let".

These provisions have been generally interpreted as having a limiting effect on the level of value which otherwise would have been achieved by the normal processes of interpretation of rental evidence.

62. It is recommended that Section 6(4) be repealed, thus permitting the valuation of dwelling-houses at current open market levels as in England and Wales. It is considered that any case which may have existed for the favourable treatment of dwelling-houses as a class for valuation purposes has been disabled by the provisions of the Rating Act, 1966, which recognises that relief from payment of rates in deserving cases is a separate matter from valuation.

Dwelling-houses occupied by crofters, cottars and small landholders

63. In the Crofting Counties, in terms of Section 7(6) of the Valuation and Rating (Scotland) Act, 1956, the rateable value of a dwelling-house occupied by a crofter, cottar or small landholder is restricted to one-half of its gross annual value. The effect of this provision is to confer on the occupiers of this class of house a measure of derating to the extent of between ten and thirty per cent compared with occupiers of similar ordinary dwelling-houses in these areas. It is recommended that this provision be discontinued. Where relief from rates is merited by the financial circumstances of the occupier, such relief is now obtainable under the provisions of the Rating Act, 1966.

Industrial and freight-transport lands and heritages

64. By Section 45 (1)(*b*) of the Local Government (Scotland) Act 1929 as amended by Section 7 of the Local Government and Miscellaneous Financial Provisions (Scotland) Act 1958, the rateable value of industrial and freight-transport lands and heritages is entered in the roll at one-half of the net annual value.

65. In terms of Section 10 of the Local Government (Financial Provisions) (Scotland) Act, 1963, the derating of industrial and freight-transport subjects should have ended on 15th May 1966. The Rating of Industry (Scotland) Order, 1965, continued this derating until the year 1971.

66. Circumstances have changed since the 1920's when industrial and freight-transport derating was initiated to reduce the rates payable by depressed industry. If the obstacles to entering dwelling-houses in the Roll at current market values are removed, and if a measure of rerating of agricultural lands and heritages is carried through, then there would be no reason for continuing industrial and freight-transport derating.

Valuation by formula of certain lands and heritages

67. Section 13 of the Local Government (Financial Provisions) (Scotland) Act, 1963, provides that the Secretary of State may by order make provision for determining by formula the rateable value of lands and heritages of certain types including—

   (i) lands and heritages occupied by the National Coal Board

   (ii) mines or quarries

   (iii) dock or harbour undertakings

   (iv) radio and television undertakings

   (v) hydro-electric power generating undertakings.

The only order so far made in terms of the powers conferred provides for the calculation by formula of the rateable values of hydro-electric power undertakings.

68. Section 24 and the Fourth Schedule of the Valuation and Rating (Scotland) Act, 1956, amended by Section 12 of the Local Government (Financial Provisions) (Scotland) Act 1963 provides for the entry in the roll of Gas Board undertakings and premises at rateable valuations in each rating area determined according to a formula set out in the Acts. The valuations are altered annually on the basis of the formula, of which the factors include the number of therms supplied by the Board in the year 1961 and the number of therms supplied in the year preceding the date of valuation. The valuations are not related to the value of property actually occupied by the Board within a local authority area. Dwelling-houses and some other types of subjects are entered in the roll at gross annual values in the ordinary way.

69. It is suggested that any provision for the valuation by formula of lands and heritages is on the whole to the financial advantage of the statutory undertakers and to the dis-advantage of rating authorities. If such arrangements are continued (in the case of existing provisions) or extended (in the case of new applications of the principle of valuation by formula), provision should be made for the frequent checking of the formula valuation against a valuation of the lands and heritages occupied by the statutory undertakers, and for consequent correction of the formula.

COMMENTS ON AREAS AND FUNCTIONS

70. As a result of the Valuation and Rating (Scotland) Act, 1956, the valuation service in Scotland is at present administered in twenty-three areas; a degree of regionalisation can therefore be said to exist. The Association is satisfied that, as regards the efficiency of the service, this enlargement of valuation areas has been of great benefit in that it has allowed the economical use of qualified and experienced staff and mechanical aids, and has enabled a much higher degree of uniformity of valuation to be achieved than would have been possible with smaller areas. No difficulties have been encountered which might have arisen from the enlargement of areas.

71. It is understood that proposals have been advanced for a substantial reduction in the number of local authorities. While from experience the Association agrees with such proposals in principle it is suggested that natural, geographical and historical associations should be taken into account and also that there is a geographical limit beyond which impairment of efficiency and service to the public would be bound to occur.

72. In order to maintain efficiency in rating it is essential that a valuer should have a good local knowledge of the area in which he works since valuations are so much influenced by and dependent upon local circumstances. The valuation function, but its nature, is one in which the actions of the responsible official bear more directly on each ratepayer than is the case with many other functions. It is therefore important to the ratepayer that he should be able to communicate with an identifiable local official, rather than with

someone whom he would regard as remote and impersonal. While an official may still be identifiable in the above sense although responsible for a fairly wide area, this advantage could be lost if excessively large areas were introduced, and the ratepayer might then feel that he was dealing with an impersonal organisation rather than a known individual.

73. While it is to the advantage of ratepayers that Assessors should be locally appointed, the full benefit of this arrangement can only be obtained if the present independence of Assessors is evident. It is essential for public confidence in the system that the Assessor should not be regarded as a government or local government official charged with the duty of increasing revenue, but should clearly be seen to be independent and impartial, subject to the decisions of Valuation Appeal Committees and the Lands Valuation Appeal Court.

74. Apart from determining the values upon which rates may be paid in respect of individual properties, the function of valuation also plays a part in determining the distribution of Exchequer equalisation grant amongst local authorities, and in providing yardsticks against which rental levels of local authority houses are judged for subsidy purposes. Recognising the necessity for a real degree of uniformity in approach to valuation problems this Association has in the past consulted together, and will continue so to consult. This indicates how a local function can be carried out independently in each area while at the same time maintaining a uniform approach with other areas, not by any specific central or statutory direction, but by means of a national association of officials working in co-operation with a body such as the Scottish Valuation Advisory Council.

75. Having regard to the wide scope of the Royal Commission's terms of reference, it was felt inappropriate to deal with certain matters in detail. The Association is willing, if called upon, to enlarge upon this memorandum and to supply any other information required by the Commission.

R. Frame (President)
T. F. Phillips (Secretary)

December, 1966.

Memorandum by the
Association of Officers of the Ministry of Labour

THE YOUTH EMPLOYMENT SERVICE

Introduction

1. The Association believes that, in the course of the comprehensive review of all aspects of Local Government administration now being undertaken by the Royal Commission, the opportunity should be taken of examining the present arrangements for providing the Youth Employment Service. Our views on this are set out below.

2. The Association represents the lower and middle management Grades in the Ministry of Labour. It therefore represents nearly all the officers who are concerned with the administration of the Youth Employment Service, both at the Ministry's Headquarters and at its Regional Offices; and about half the Ministry of Labour's 220 Youth Employment Officers. (The remainder are represented by the Ministry of Labour Staff Association, a body with whom we have a very close relationship). The Association is therefore in a unique position to comment on this matter, as it is the only independent body with members at all levels of Youth Employment Service.

Brief History

3. The Youth Employment Service as a national undertaking began about the same time as the adult employment service, in 1910, though semi-voluntary arrangements had been in operation in a few areas before that date. But whereas the adult employment service was operated as a national entity from the start, first under the Board of Trade and later under the Ministry of Labour, this has never been the case with the Youth Employment Service, which at all periods of its history has been more or less unhappily split in its operation between Education (mainly through Local Education Authorities) and Employment (through the Ministry of Labour). The matter has been examined at various times since 1910, and a variety of solutions has been tried; but all have been more or less dictated by expediency, and none has proved to be without the most serious drawbacks. The last two reviews were carried out by a Committee under the Chairmanship of Sir Godfrey Ince (which reported in September, 1945), and by a Working Party of the National Youth Employment Council under the Chairmanship of Lady Albemarle (which reported in September, 1965). We shall be referring to these two reports as "The Ince Report" and "The Albemarle Report".

4. It is not the intention of the Association in this paper to go into detail of the history of the Youth Employment Service; an excellent summary is contained in the Ince Report, paragraphs 7–22. Suffice it to say that from its inception, the Youth Employment Service has been performed in certain areas by local Education Authorities, and over the remainder of the country by the Ministry of Labour. Prior to the Employment and Training Act, 1948, (which gave effect to those of the recommendations of the Ince Committee which were adopted), there were no common standards of performance and no stability of organisation, since any Local Education Authority could decide to perform the Service, or to hand it back to the Ministry, on giving three months notice. The Employment and Training Act, 1948, attempted to introduce stability by giving Local Education Authorities a once-for-all option to provide the Service, and to introduce equality of standard by the provision in the Ministry of Labour of a central Inspectorate. In the 18 years that have elapsed since the Act took effect there have been definite improvements in the service from all points of view.

5. The present position is that, of 196 Local Education Authorities, 144 have elected to provide a Youth Employment Service, and 52 have not. The 144 comprise most of the main centres of population, and between them they deal with about 84% of all school leavers. The areas where the Service is provided by the Ministry include most of the scattered rural areas which are generally difficult to administer. The Local Education Authorities employ some 1,320 Youth Employment Officers (including many who are wholly engaged in the administration of the Service in their areas); the Ministry has about 220.

6. Over the years several attempts have been made to examine and evaluate the dual system of administration which has prevailed since the inception of the Service. All have failed to resolve the difficulty, largely because nearly all the parties who gave evidence had vested interests in the continuance of one or the other type of administration. The Association regrets to say that in this process the best interests of the child were more often than not forgotten. It now appears that the Albemarle Report and the report of the present Royal Commission may determine the pattern of the Youth Employment Service for many years to come. The Association hopes that the opportunity will be taken to examine the matter afresh, untrammelled by vested interests or by past mistakes.

The Function of the Youth Employment Service

7. The main functions of the Youth Employment Service with the individual young person are well described in Chapter 11 of the Albemarle Report. Briefly, they are:—

  (i) to help to introduce him to "the world of work", giving in the process information which will enable him to play his part in the subsequent guidance;

  (ii) to guide him in his choice of career in accordance with his interests, aptitudes and abilities;

  (iii) to find him work in accordance with that guidance, and to ensure that he is settled in it.

8. The Service also has responsibilities to parents, who must be consulted and informed as fully as possible; and to industry, to whom it is responsible for the supply of young workers. There are also special responsibilities to those young people who need special help by virtue of physical, mental, or environmental handicap, and to those who have attained higher educational qualifications.

9. It will be noted that the first function referred to in paragraph 7 is performed almost entirely in schools and is predominantly educational; while the second must also be performed before the child leaves school. This latter can, however, be performed only by someone with a detailed knowledge of industry; while the work of introduction must also at least be planned in conjunction with such a person. On the other hand, once the young person has left school and has started work, the task of dealing with him becomes purely occupational. It is unlikely that these basic functions will change in the foreseeable future, and we must therefore consider who is best fitted to undertake each one.

The introductory work in schools

10. There is no doubt that the most important development in recent years has been the great increase in the number of Careers Teachers, and the inception of proper courses of training for them. The desired goal will obviously be for every school from which young people will leave to enter employment to have a trained careers teacher, with an allowance for a post of special responsibility, a definite allocation of time in which to perform careers duties, and a room in the school in which booklets and other literature may be displayed, and interviews given.

11. It would be quite wrong, however, to train a teacher in this way and then limit his work to miscellaneous advice (as happens in many schools today). If the school's careers programme is to be an integral, living part of the curriculum of the final years*, it must be best performed by a member of the school staff. But it remains true that the careers teacher cannot be an expert on everything; he will need outside advice on industrial matters, and this is properly the function of the Youth Employment Officer.

12. This distinction is referred to several times in the Albemarle Report. The Association of Educational Committees is quoted† as saying that the careers master is concerned with the general picture and the Y.E.O. with narrowing matters to a decision. The Head-masters' Association saw "the careers master as an amateur on careers but an expert on boys; the Y.E.O. vice versa"; and the National Union of Teachers also distinguished between the school's knowledge of the pupil and the Y.E.O.'s knowledge of occupations‡.

13. It appears therefore that the consensus of educational opinion is that in connection with his work in schools the Y.E.O. must be primarily an expert on industry in its widest sense. Naturally, he must also have a close acquaintance with education, but all appear to regard that as the secondary requirement.

The Vocational Guidance Interview

14. This interview has always been regarded as the primary function of a Y.E.O. It is, indeed, quite proper that it should be so regarded; the preparatory work in schools exists only so that the young person may be properly informed for his interview with the Y.E.O. and for his subsequent entry into work; the placing and, later, the follow-up, only give effect to the guidance and ensure that any mistakes made on either side are quickly rectified. But the interview is the climax of the Y.E.O.'s activity. For it is essential that he should be able to establish quickly an understanding with every young person; he should meet him as a friend, not as a stranger. Once again it appears that the main contribution the Y.E.O. can make to the interview, apart from his skill in guidance techniques, is an intimate knowledge of industry, and, of course, of higher opportunities available after courses of further education. With the help of the school, it will not in most cases be difficult to determine the young person's interests, aptitudes and abilities: but only a wide and detailed acquaintance with jobs will equate those qualities with the right opening or course.

Placing and subsequent action

15. Up to now we have considered the Y.E.O. in his liaison with schools; from now on his work will be in liaison with industry. He becomes equally the servant of industry and of the young person. And, from the very moment that the young person starts work, he has become a member of the nation's manpower machine. From that moment onwards, and increasingly as time goes by, he will find that his interests march much more with those of his fellow-workers than with those of his former school-fellows. The Y.E.O. can make an effective first placing in employment, and can guide the young worker effectively through the many difficulties that may beset him in the early stages of his working life, only if he has a detailed knowledge of industry, of industrial training methods, of trade unions, and of many incidental matters besides. Moreover, if he is to gain and retain the confidence of the employers whom he is to serve, he must have an intimate understanding of their methods and their needs.

The Pattern of the future

16. It appears to the Association, therefore, that the Youth Employment Service has reached a stage in its development where it is about to undergo a fundamental change.

---

* Albemarle Report, paras. 29 et seq.
† Ibid, para. 20.
  Ibid, para. 21.

Hitherto it has been a service whose links with the education have been at least as important as those with industry; many have considered the educational links to predominate. But it is apparent that this is so, not because this was the proper field of activity for the Service, but because education had not provided any means of meeting the need from within its own boundaries. Few schools had appointed careers teachers; few had any idea of the responsibilities of the school in helping young people towards employment. Even now many teachers express the view that their function is education alone, and that the job of introduction to work belongs to someone else. This idea is, however, rapidly losing ground, and publications such as the Department of Education and Science's "Careers Works in Schools" can only speed the change.

17. The pattern of the future, therefore, emerges clearly. The introductory and preparatory work will in future be done by the school and by teachers, with the Y.E.O. as an industrial adviser and occasional participant; the Vocational Guidance work will be the Y.E.O.'s own field, but it will be greatly simplified if the preparatory work has been of a high quality: and the placing and after care will naturally fall to him, simply because he has known the young person throughout his transition from school to work. The predominantly industrial content of the job in such a context is manifest.

18. It must be a matter of grave doubt whether such a Service could any longer be run by a body whose primary duty is education. It must equally be a matter of grave doubt whether a Service which must be national in basis and performance could any longer be effectively performed by local authorities. In the next section we examine some of the difficulties which local administration has caused, and indeed, continues to cause.

An Examination of Local Authority Administration of the Service

19. The first difficulty concerns the effect of local authority boundaries on the organisation of the Service. These boundaries are not drawn with industrial and employment needs in mind; there is no reason why they should be, since—apart from this one small sector— local authorities have no industrial and employment responsibilities. Examples of cases where the main centre of employment is in the area of one local authority and a major area of residence in another are too numerous to mention. This would not matter if local authorities were prepared to work effectively with each other, but the Association is aware of several cases where such co-operation is minimal or almost non-existent, resulting in inequality of employment opportunity between children from the "employer" area and those from the "fringe" dormitory area. The evils of this are too obvious to require comment, and the problem is sufficiently widespread to be a serious one.

20. Despite efforts by the Inspectorate of the Central Youth Employment Executive, it has proved impossible to produce anything like a uniform standard of efficiency among the 144 Local Education Authority Services. The Association is aware of many excellent Services; but it is also aware of many only barely above the borderline of efficiency, and a few actually below it. It believes that it must be a cardinal principle of any national Employment Service, that while permitting local variations to meet local needs, it must maintain a uniform standard of efficiency; that the quality of service should not vary because of the accident of where a young person happens to live, or where an employer's premises happen to be situated. The Association is aware of many examples of these differences, and considers them to be a grave indictment of local authority administration.

21. The Local Authority Service is permanently understaffed. It is difficult to determine the extent of this, though the Association believes it to be of the order of 10% to 15%; since, apparently, it is only exceptionally possible to fill all the long-term training places available, this under-staffing looks like becoming a chronic state. Naturally, the geographically "unpopular" parts of the country fare worse in this, and many authorities are forced to fill their vacancies with staff of inferior quality, making a further contribution to the inequality of the Service already noted.

22. The willingness of local authorities to send their Officers to training courses varies greatly. Some are both generous and enlightened; others frankly parsimonious or unwilling to recognise the need. The Service is developing so quickly that only by regular refresher and similar training can all be kept in touch, and again local administration provides a clear barrier.

23. The Albemarle Working Party noted the need for a national agreement on scales for posts of comparable responsibility. The Association points out that because of the absence of such an agreement a sort of auction is in progress, in which even new entrants to the Service without previous experience are demanding to start near the maximum of the scale offered. With certain authorities apparently willing to accede to these demands, the chances of authorities unable or unwilling to do so of getting staff are correspondingly diminished. Whatever the rights and wrongs of this situation, it cannot be denied that it also contributes to the inequalities of the Service.

24. The Association considers that, whatever the ultimate organisation of the Youth Employment Service may be, it is no longer possible to permit it to operate at such widely differing levels of efficiency, of staffing, or of training, as those that have been described. If it is to be left in the hands of local authorities, some more effective means of ensuring common standards must be found than that at present provided. But since enforcement is likely to be both difficult and slow, whatever means of this type may be designed, it appears that serious consideration should now be given to the possibility of producing a truly national Service. Only in this way can the Youth Employment Service escape from the web of administrative complications which have beset it ever since its inception; only in this way can any guarantee be given that the recommendations of the Albemarle Working Party will be carried out with equal enthusiasm in all areas—or even that they will be carried out at all.

The Advantages of a National Service

25. The advantages of a national service would be many. Because it would embrace posts at local, regional, and national level, it would provide a career structure which would encourage men and women of ability to join it. They could make it a life's career, or could come into it on secondment for more limited terms from many walks of life. By looking at the position nationally, it would be possible to avoid staffing inequalities, both in number and in quality. It would be possible to ensure proper training at all levels and in all areas. The areas of the different offices would be delineated with the sole object of equating as best may be the "supplying" schools with the "employing" industry and commerce. And the Service would gain in status and reputation from the very fact that it was a national and specialist organisation.

26. Perhaps almost as important as these considerations would be the increased efficiency that would result. At present, a great deal of time and money is employed simply in trying to arrange some form of co-ordination between local authorities of many different types, and with as many local policies. This expenditure of effort is inherent in any attempt to run a national Service on a system of delegation to local bodies. There are a number of ways in which new techniques, especially in the mechanisation of office work, could be used if the basic organisation were of a type to permit them.

27. The object of the adoption of such more modern and efficient methods of administration is not for efficiency's sake alone, but also to release scarce qualified manpower for more effective work. Indeed the whole purpose behind the Association's proposals is to ensure that each part of the job of transferring a young person form school to work is done by the body best able and best trained to do it; and it is our submission that this can be attained in no other way.

Responsibility for the Service

28. The Association realises that a recommendation as to which Minister of State should have ultimate responsibility to Parliament for the Youth Employment Service is not within the terms of reference for the Royal Commission. It feels, however, that it must make a brief statement on the point, as only in this way can a complete picture be drawn.

29. The Minister of Labour (and prior to the establishment of that Ministry, the President of the Board of Trade) has always had the main responsibility to Parliament for the Service. But for a period up to 1927, the President of the Board of Education (as the post was then called) was responsible to Parliament for those parts of the Service performed by Local Education Authorities. This arrangement proved unsatisfactory to the highest degree.

30. If it be admitted (and no recent pronouncement to the subject has even hinted at a contrary view) that the main responsibility of Youth Employment Service is to guide each young person into that employment in which he can best use his abilities, aptitudes and interests, after further education if appropriate, and that all other activities are merely preparatory or confirmatory, then it is clear that the Ministry of Labour is the only Department of State under which such a Service can operate. To suggest, as some do, that it could be controlled by the Department of Education and Science, is an error arising from the assumption that the Service must always remain educationally based; and it is a suggestion which would only add to administrative difficulty. It would mean duplicating within the Department of Education and Science facilities for the clearing over the whole country of vacancies and of details of young persons seeking work away from home, facilities for the processing and analysis of statistics, facilities for special assistance to the handicapped and disabled, expert advice on wages and allied matters—indeed, most of the services provided by the Ministry of Labour which Youth Employment Officers, especially those employed by local authorities, take for granted at present. We think, too, that there has never been a proper appreciation in Education Authorities of the extent to which their work in the Youth Employment Service is facilitated by, and, indeed, even is dependent on, the contacts with firms at all levels, with trade unions, and with organisations of employers, which have been maintained by the Ministry of Labour over many years.

Conclusion

31. To sum up, then, there seems to be no doubt that the Youth Employment Service of the future will need the closest of contacts with industry, at every level of operation. The Association considers that it would be impossible to establish such a service on any other basis than that of a national organisation closely linked to the Ministry of Labour. It hopes that the Royal Commission will endorse this view.

Addendum

32. The Association realises that the very brief historical summary in this paper does not take account of the fact that the history of the Youth Employment Service in Scotland differs from that in England. In Scotland, prior to the passing of the Employment and Training Act of 1948, Education Authorities had never had an option of performing the Youth Employment Service, and the whole of it was undertaken by the Ministry of Labour. The Ince Report recommended that such an option should be given (although a minority report from a Scottish member opposed this recommendation, on the ground that Scotland should not be subjected to the disadvantages of dual administration); and the option was given in the Employment and Training Act. The system of dual control in Scotland dates therefore only from 1948.

Memorandum by the
Institute of Weights and Measures Administration

Summary of Recommendations

1. This Institute is of the opinion that any consideration as to the placing of the weights and measures service within any specific unit of local government should be based on the following principles:—

Weights and Measures Departments should be large enough to:—

    (a) justify the employment of a reasonable number of inspectors;

    (b) be able to afford the more costly equipment required to test and check the extensive additional items introduced by the Weights and Measures Act, 1963.

    (c) be able to provide adequate training facilities for future inspectors.

    (d) comprise a Department of Consumer and Public Protection Services combining the enforcement of analogous statutes.

    (e) undertake the costly sampling, test purchasing, analysis or testing of goods envisaged by the Protection of Consumers (Trade Descriptions) Bill.

2. The advantages of combining consumer and protective responsibilities in the same hands are:—

    (a) to minimise the number of enforcement officers;

    (b) to facilitate the introduction of co-ordinated schemes for selective sampling and test-purchasing of nationally distributed goods;

    (c) to reduce the number of officials visiting trade premises since inspections under a number of Acts can be carried out at one and the same time;

    (d) to concentrate in one department the place to which the public can direct enquiries and complaints and where traders can obtain advice.

Introduction

3. The White Paper issued in 1963 by the Scottish Development Department on the modernisation of Local Government in Scotland (Cmnd. 2067) proposed a two tier authority system, placing weights and measures initially in the lower tier.

4. After submissions by various associations, and examination by the Working Party set up by the White Paper, there was drawn up the First Report of the Working Party (published in 1964) which listed a number of functions whose allocation to a particular tier leaves no real room for doubt, and which submitted that the weights and measures service should be allotted to the first tier.

5. A complete enquiry into the service is contained in the Report of the Committee on Weights and Measures Legislation (Cmd 8219/1951—known as the Hodgson Report). The Weights and Measures Act, 1963, is based largely on the recommendations of the Hodgson Committee, but, in specifying the local Weights and Measures Authorities in Scotland, it departed from the Hodgson recommendation by allowing the Council of a County or Large Burgh to be a Weights and Measures Authority. It recognised that some of these were too small for the purpose by introducing in Section 37, powers to combine for all or any of their functions under the Act.

6. A system of voluntary combination of authorities has built up over the years and the retention of these combinations as authorised in the Act has continued to be present. The 33 County Councils operate 22 Weights and Measures Departments, and, of the 20 Large Burghs, 12 are amalgamated or joined with their respective County Councils. This practice of voluntary combination is a clear indication that a number of local authorities consider themselves too small to provide an effective service at reasonable cost.

7. The effect of the Weights and Measures Act, 1963, has been to widen the scope of enforcement. Originally, Inspectors were concerned mainly with maintaining uniform units of weight and measure and testing and stamping equipment for use for trade, and for ensuring that such equipment remained correct within tolerance. Gradually the check-weighing and measuring of some commodities was added until now, all commodities sold by weight and measure are controlled and many which were previously sold "by the packet" are now required to be sold by weight and measure.

Practical difficulties within the existing structure

8. The pattern of trading has altered considerably in that, whereas formerly, most goods were weighed or measured in the premises in which they were sold, now, the bulk of commodities are pre-packed and weighed in factories. This has resulted in weighing and measuring equipment becoming complex and automated, requiring special equipment for checking certain products. The existing structure is such that it is uneconomic for individual authorities to provide for their own use, heavy weighbridge testing equipment and proving tanks, etc. While an attempt has been made in certain areas to overcome the difficulties by conjoining with neighbouring authorities in the provision of heavy testing equipment, the whole country is not covered by such schemes to the detriment of maintaining a uniform standard of service.

9. Where the area is small or compact, difficulties are experienced in checking supplies of goods by vendors operating from mobile premises. The vendor is often aware of the inspector's movements and can recognise him more easily to allow of evasive action being taken to move over the boundary and out of the inspector's jurisdiction. Note:—Section 48(7) of the Act states, "Nothing in this Act shall authorise any inspector to stop any vehicle on a highway".

10. The training of future inspectors is most easily carried out in units in which there is a sufficient variety of equipment to give candidates a good all-round experience. The training must, of course, be supplemented by a proper course of training at which assistants can attend on a day release or residential basis without their absence seriously affecting the day-to-day running of the Department.

11. All but one of the Weights and Measures Departments in Scotland enforce other statutes of a consumer protection nature (see Appendix II). Unfortunately there is no uniformity. The legislation can be divided into two main groups—that of a direct consumer nature which can be subdivided into (1) value for money and (2) safety—and those miscellaneous functions which are in some ways analogous to consumer services, and are administered by Weights and Measures and other Departments as an administrative convenience, and described briefly as ancillary services.

Consumer Services

Value for money

Weights and Measures
Food and Drugs
Merchandise Marks
Fertiliser and Feeding Stuffs
Agricultural Produce

Safety

Petroleum
Explosives
Pharmacy and Poisons
Consumer Protection
Fabrics Misdescription
Road Traffic (Section 221/1960)

Ancillary Services

Shops
Road Traffic (section 224/1960)
Young Persons Employment
Vehicles Excise—Taxation weighing

12. Each of these services has been created independently without planned direction as to the hands into which enforcement should go and the duties have been put diversely upon the different types of local authorities. Even when one type of authority is charged with a number of the duties, there is no uniformity as to the appropriate disposition of them between departments. There is no co-ordinated pattern within individual authorities, the duties being scattered among Weights and Measures, Sanitary Inspectors', Police, and, in one instance Fire Departments. It would be to the ultimate benefit of the community and the local government service as a whole, if these services were integrated within the Weights and Measures Department into a single all-purpose department of consumer and public protection services.

13. The field of consumer protection was considered by the Molony Committee in their Report to Parliament (Cmnd. 1781/1962) on the extension and strengthening of the Merchandise Marks Acts. To enforce the new legislation outlined in the Report, para. 682 states:—"The local authorities given this mandate should be those concerned with weights and measures responsibility on the assumption that this responsibility will reside in the largest units of local government. Without having made a close study of the matter we express the opinion that the advantage of combining weights and measures and food and drugs together with Merchandise Marks enforcement responsibility in the same hands is sufficiently obvious in principle to be worked for."

14. The Molony Committee Report led to the Protection of Consumers (Trade Descriptions) Bill, designed to replace existing legislation relating to Merchandise Marks. It was introduced into the last Parliament and was progressing through the Lords at the dissolution. The Government has stated its intention to re-introduce it whenever time is available. The Bill imposed the duty of enforcement on Weights and Measures Authorities.

15. The purpose of this Bill, had it become law, was to make Weights and Measures Authorities responsible for the supervision of all trade description of goods as to quantity, size, gauge, method of manufacture, composition, fitness for purpose, strength, performance, accuracy, physical characteristics, testing by any person and the results thereof, place or date of manufacture and persons by whom manufactured, and other history including previous ownership and use. Trade Description included advertisements and oral statements and services were dealt with in addition to goods.

16. It is obvious that enforcement of such provisions would be costly requiring selective sampling and test purchasing followed by either submission to analysts or testing houses, or the provision by local authorities themselves of testing laboratories for checking that claims made by sellers of goods were justified.

Proposals for Reform—Department of Consumer Services

17. Appendix I sets out a summary of (*a*) Consumer and (*b*) Ancillary legislation.

18. The functions are unified in concept, purpose and practical enforcement. They impose a common basic correctness in the essential attributes of goods on sale so that the consumer is protected from fraud, unfairness and hazard. They regulate statements of quantity, substance and quality where such are material characteristics, they challenge the shady misuse of nomenclature and debasement of known names and terms, they protect the consumer's pocket; they guard him from danger, they enable him to know what he is getting and to evaluate between comparable articles on sale. They protect the fair trader from his dishonest or negligent rival.

19. Throughout, there are common factors pointing to the need for unified direction:—

(*a*) Each function is expressed in legislation of the same structure, consisting of general prohibitions with detailed prescriptions of control expressed in regulations.

(*b*) Enforcement involves frequent inspection of traders premises and practices. There is the same selection of samples and test purchasing, the same enquiries, assembly of data and evidence and the same continued enforcement by way of advice, guidance, caution and prosecution.

(*c*) Each function deals with characteristics of consumer goods and the behaviour of persons selling the goods or with safety standards and control of dangerous substances. Each in various ways requires the same high degree of technical knowledge as to the goods, the equipment and the trade practice.

(*d*) These various inspections, purchases, enquiries, guidance, negotiations, prosecutions and general dealings with trade can really coincide at one time under various duties upon one trader in respect of one article. Unification of enforcement is desirable not only to the local government service but also to the trader and the ratepayer. It is illogical for officers of different departments to visit the same trade premises for purposes sufficiently akin to one another when they can all be dealt with at the same time.

(*e*) Primarily inspection in each service is undertaken in trade premises. The advantages of combining routine inspection under the various duties at one time is that enforcement rests with the same department thereby achieving economies in manpower, the reduction of overall travelling time, and, of primary importance, reduces the number of visits by different officials to busy retail and manufacturing premises.

(*f*) Each service demands the same continual relationship with the public, traders, trade associations and government departments. Obviously unified enforcement is of the greatest benefit in saving the time of all concerned. This is particularly so in the case of the public who find it frustrating to be referred from one department to another when seeking information or redress in some matter.

(*g*) Officers must, in all cases, acquire an intimate knowledge of traders and of trade practices and commerce in a wide range of goods. The problems of one service may well have a bearing upon another. The decisions of the Courts in one sphere often affect the others. Overall the officers must possess the same amalgam of legal—technical—administrative knowledge and skill.

(*h*) In each case Officers must be impartial to all and must be fortified by the support of a sufficiently large local authority. Enforcement, now more than ever, is concerned with distribution and advertising extending over an ever increasing area. It is necessary therefore for enforcement to be geared to these factors otherwise there is duplication of duties and effort, duplication of office accommodation and clerical staff, variable treatment of the same trade or an ineffectual enforcement.

(*i*) The most effective deterrent to transgression is the knowledge of active, impartial and uniform enforcement which, as well as achieving considerable saving in cost and time and an increase in efficiency, eliminates confusion to traders.

Units of Administration and Enforcement

20. It is not the purpose of the memorandum to make suggestions as to the form and most appropriate unit of local government as a whole but to submit proposals in relation to the existing Weights and Measures Service and the recommended Department of Consumer Services. It is considered that the White Paper issued in 1963 by the Scottish Development Department on the Modernisation of Local Government in Scotland (Cmnd. 2067) and the First Report by the Working Party set up by the White Paper does provide some guidance in this field.

Appendix 1

SUMMARY OF CONSUMER AND OTHER LEGISLATION

Consumer Protection

Value for Money

Weights and Measures

1. The functions of this old and vital service are basically threefold: first, the standardisation of units of weights and measure to ensure the exchange of goods by means of true quantity; secondly, the control of weighing and measuring equipment in use for trade; thirdly, the control of sale of goods in terms of quantity, to enable evaluation to be made and to prevent short quantity on sale.

2. The first function historically has been difficult to achieve but has now been accomplished. The second function involves the examination, verification and stamping of all apparatus before it is put into use; it also involves visits of inspection to trade premises where such equipment is used to ensure that it is still accurate and is not being misused. The third function is control over the quantity of goods sold, extending not merely to verbal representations but also to those written or printed on labels, invoices or in advertisements, and applies to foods and to non-foods. So far as sales of commodities subject to the law are concerned, checks must be made of delivery vehicles and the purported quantities of the articles in or on them. In shops, two main methods of inspection are required. First, there are all goods which are pre-packed by remote manufacturers or are imported. Here, if fault is found in weight or measure, it will usually be traced back through the channel of distribution to the original manufacturer or importer, with either of whom (in the case of pre-packed goods) responsibility generally will lie, and here the inspection can usually be overt; secondly, articles which are weighed or measured by the shopkeeper must be checked and faults discovered rest with him. For these checks it may be necessary to make purchases.

3. The exercise of these weights and measures functions requires scientific and technical knowledge; the maintenance of elaborate equipment; the absorption of technical and trade information; constant supervision of traders of every description; and the oversight of the apparatus they use and the goods they sell.

Food and Drugs

4. The Food and Drugs Acts confer separate functions on two distinct authorities; the "local authority", for functions akin to the safeguarding of public health, and the "food and drugs authority". It is with the duties of the latter that we are concerned. The objects of these duties are primarily to ensure that foods and drugs which are sold are genuine, that foods are accurately labelled as to their designation and composition, that foods do not contain unlawful substances and that labels and advertisements relating to foods and drugs are not false or misleading.

5. The act of debasing a food or drug with the object of passing it off as genuine or the substitution of an inferior article for a superior one to the detriment of the purchaser, whether done in fraud or negligence, appears to be as old as trade. These practices have led to official suppressive action (by the twin needs to protect the purchaser and the honest trader). The Acts, therefore, contain broad and simple prohibitions—for example, the preparations and sale of injurious foods and adulterated drugs; the sale of foods and drugs not of the nature or substance or quality that the purchaser is deemed to expect; the false or misleading labelling or advertising of a food or drug. To meet the revolutionary growth of compound foods and the distribution of pre-packed articles in huge quantities, control by regulations is provided as to the composition, labelling, marking and advertising of foods. Enforcement involves a knowledge of the articles of food and drugs on sale and of selective sampling. Having regard to modern distribution of goods in processing, pre-packing and multiple shop distribution, steps must be taken to avoid unnecessary duplication of sampling.

6. The essential difference between the duties of the "food and drugs authority" and those of a "local authority" under the Food and Drugs Acts are emphasised by the clear separation with which they are treated in the Acts as well as by the prior history of these separate functions. Food and drugs duties are aimed at the protection of the purchaser and shield him against the adulteration and substitution or passing-off of a commodity of a different kind or inferior quality from the one declared or demanded, and from false or misleading descriptions or claims. The "local authority" has quite separate and different functions under the Act, being concerned with such matters as unsound or decomposed food, suitability of premises used for food storage and preparation, and the registration of dairymen and matters of hygiene control. Public health matters are purely local in nature, dealing with persons, premises and practices on an intimate scale: food and drugs (as with the other consumer protection services) is a duty more appropriately dealt with by independent officers remote from local influence, with trade which is not merely parochial but widespread.

Merchandise Marks

7. The Merchandise Marks Acts prohibit the application to goods in trade of written descriptions which are false or misleading in a material respect, as to either the number, quantity, measure, gauge, weight, material, quality (according to a trade classification), fitness for purpose, strength, performance or behaviour, place or country of production, mode of manufacture or production. They also prohibit various trade dealings in goods which have such offending descriptions applied to them by label, invoice or advertisement.

8. An Act of 1926 provides for the making of Imported Goods Marking Orders. These apply to a wide range of goods and include goods such as meat, offals, fresh apples, honey, raw tomatoes, eggs in shell, certain dried fruits, dead poultry, butter, bacon and ham. Their effect, when in force, is to protect home and importing traders, as well as the consumer-purchaser, by requiring that these goods, if imported, be marked on sale with the words "Empire" or "Foreign" (as appropriate) or specifically with their country of origin. The enforcement of the food Orders is permissive upon food and drugs authorities.

The biggest defect in all this lesiglation is that there is no mandatory duty of enforcement put upon anybody. Local authorities, by virtue of the Local Government Act, 1933, may prosecute any proceedings taken in the protection of the interests of their inhabitants and the overwhelming proportion of prosecutions under the main Acts are undertaken by such authorities, particularly through their Weights and Measures Department. The Protection of Consumers (Trade Descriptions) Bill, if enacted will extend the provisions of the Merchandise Marks Act considerably and will make Local Weights and Measures Authorities the enforcing authorities.

Fertiliser and Feeding Stuffs

9. Present law is contained in the Fertilisers and Feeding Stuffs Act of 1926 and the Fertilisers and Feeding Stuffs Regulations of 1960, although the control started in 1893. The Act provides for civil action to be taken, in prescribed cases, by an aggrieved purchaser, but it is with the criminal provisions which are enforced by local authorities through inspectors appointed under the Act that we are concerned.

10. The duty is placed upon the seller of a scheduled fertiliser or feeding stuff (whatever may be the name under which the article is sold) to give the purchaser a statement in writing containing;

(*a*) the name under which the article is sold;

(*b*) particulars if any, of the nature, substance or quality of the article;

(*c*) in the case of a feeding stuff which contains any ingredients included in the third schedule to the regulations the name of such ingredient.

11. There are requirements for labelling with the statutory statement, articles exposed for sale. Offences are committed under the Act if these requirements are not met or if, on analysis, it appears that the particulars marked or indicated by a mark are false to the prejudice of the purchaser. Inspectors appointed by the local authority under the Act have power of entry to premises and powers of sampling to enforce the Act. The level of enforcement of the Act by local authorities varies widely throughout the country. It is important that there should be more uniformity and a reasonable number of samples be procured.

Agricultural Produce (*Grading and Marking*)

12. This legislation provides for the Minister of Agriculture, Fisheries and Food to make regulations prescribing appropriate grade designations to indicate the quality of any agricultural, horticultural or fishery produce; which includes all articles of food or drink wholly or partly manufactured therefrom and fleeces and skins of animals. Such "grade designation" statutorily defines the quality of any particular produce.

Safety

Petroleum

13. The Petroleum (Regulation) Acts, 1928 and 1936, provide a measure of public protection against hazard in the storage, packaging, handling and conveyance by road of such dangerous goods as petrol, petroleum mixtures including cellulose, cellulose fillers, spirit varnishes, polishes, adhesives, industrial solvents, paints, printing inks, rubber solutions, carbide of calcium, acetylene and numerous other products, and also, when a licence to store ceases, to ensure that the premises are returned to a safe condition.

14. The practical work involved includes the licensing of installations, revision of the conditions under which licences are granted, keeping detailed records thereof and inspection of premises. It is generally accepted that all premises should be visited at least twice in each year; where necessary, tests for explosive atmospheres should be made and the condition of installations and of types of materials used should be constantly reviewed. In addition, petrol tankers are subject to structural requirements and must be inspected and a tighter regular supervision must be made of bulk deliveries. These are regulations which must, in the public interest, be rigidly enforced and their breach owing to the frailty of human nature is not infrequent. Inspection necessitates entry into garages, filling stations, wholesale distributing depots, factories and retail shops to name but a few types of premises involved.

Explosives

15. The safety function of local authorities under the Explosives Acts, 1875 and 1923 imposes duties upon handlers requiring that explosives be kept (*a*) in proper form, (*b*) in limited quantities, (*c*) in a safe manner and (*d*) only in registered or licensed premises: or (*e*) be conveyed safely. The law is again in the guise of absolute prohibition and is detailed and complex. Nearly all premises which have to be visited under the Explosives Acts are also visited for Weights and Measures purposes.

Pharmacy and Poisons

16. The Pharmacy and Poisons Act, 1933, has a two-fold purpose: first, to establish the law relating to the practice of the profession of pharmacy and secondly, to regulate the sale of poisons. The regulation of pharmacists and their sales is a matter for the Pharmaceutical Society of Great Britain, but, under the Act, local authorities have certain responsibilities in relation to the sale of some poisons and it is with this duty that we are concerned. The law permits certain poisonous substances (e.g. domestic, horticultural, hair-dressing preparations) to be sold by retail dealers who are not chemists provided such persons are registered with the local authority in whose area they trade. The type of container used and its labelling and, in some cases, storage, are subject to control. There are also in respect of sales of more dangerous poisons, particularly arsenical and mercuric fungicides and insecticides, restrictions upon sale which include the seller's knowledge of the purchaser and the keeping of a Poisons Book. This work gives rise to certain practical duties which include: (*a*) maintenance of a list of sellers, (*b*) inspection of premises, (*c*) sampling and (*d*) test-purchasing.

Consumer Protection

17. There is a certain amount of legislation regarding the safety of specific appliances. The Consumer Protection Act, 1961, empowered the Home Secretary to make regulations with respect to safety requirements and instructions for any prescribed class of goods and raised prohibitions of absolute liability on the seller of non-complying articles and the duty of enforcement upon particular local authorities. These include:—

   (*a*) The Heating Appliances (Fire Guards) Regulations, 1953, which require, subject to exemptions, that gas fires, electric fires and oil heaters be fitted with fireguards which are so designed that they are suitable for use in residential premises.

   (*b*) The Oil Heater Regulations, 1962, which prescribe standards of construction, design and performance for all unflued domestic oil heaters manufactured after 1st June, 1962, and sold or held for sale.

(c) The Childrens Nightdresses Regulations, 1964, require nightdresses for children to be made of fabrics of low flammability. Technical specifications set out the permitted degrees of flammability and it is an offence to sell articles not conforming with the specification.

Fabrics (Misdescription) Act

18. This Act imposes upon certain local authorities the duty of enforcing the provisions of the Act which prohibit the sale, exposure for sale or having in possession for sale of any textile fabric to which is attributed the quality of safety from fire unless the fabric conforms with the prescribed standard of non-flammability.

Road Traffic (Protective Helmets for motor cyclists)

19. Of the same nature but historically coming under Section 221 of the Road Traffic Act, 1960, is the prescription that all motor cyclists' protective helmets must conform with a standard of safety prescribed by the British Standards Institution. Enforcement is by visits to shops for the purpose of examination of these articles on sale and involves sampling and testing.

Miscellaneous

Shops

Young Persons Employment

20. Shops Act and associated legislation deals in the main with the closing of shops on weekdays and Sundays, the conditions of employment of shop assistants, the hours of employment of young persons working in shops. The provisions are extended in certain respects to places other than shops and to certain young persons who are not strictly "shop assistants" within the primary meaning given to the term in the Act. The purpose of the law in this regard is to hold and to maintain a just balance between the legitimate and reasonable demands of three sections of the community, namely, employers/employees and the purchasing public. It seeks by governing the hours of retail trade, (i) to ensure that so far as possible no real element of unfair competition shall be allowed to develop, (ii) to procure for employees reasonable opportunity for recreation, rest and study and (iii) to allow the purchasing public reasonable opportunity to get goods they require. In addition, there is a purpose to govern to some degree conditions of employment.

Road Traffic (Heavily laden vehicles)

21. The duties arising under section 224 of the Road Traffic Act, 1960, permit the authorisation of a person by a highway authority to stop and weigh any vehicle used on a road to ensure that the weight transferred to the road surface by the wheels does not infringe the maximum weight set out in regulations made under the Act. The purpose is to curtail dangerous overloading and primarily to protect road surfaces from undue wear.

Motor Vehicles (Local Taxation Weighing)

22. The Vehicle (Excise) Act, 1949, and the Regulations of 1955 made thereunder require a declaration of unladen weight in respect of new vehicles or old vehicles within seven days. This is a local taxation matter, but the purpose being that duty is paid according to weight, there arises in this circumscribed area the necessity to weigh vehicles and to examine them to ensure that they comply with the requirements of unladen weight; that is to say, a scrutiny of contents of the radiator and fuel sump, of tools and of movable fittings has to be made.

Appendix 2

LOCAL WEIGHTS AND MEASURES AUTHORITIES IN SCOTLAND AND FUNCTIONS ADDITIONAL TO WEIGHTS AND MEASURES

	Food and Drugs	Merchandise Marks	Fertiliser and feeding Stuffs	Agricultural Produce	Petroleum	Explosives	Pharmacy and Poisons	Consumer and Protection	Fabrics Misdescription	Road Traffic Section 221/60	Celluloid and Cinematograph Shops Act	Road Traffic Section 224/60	Young Persons Employment	Vehicles—Taxation Weighing
Counties														
Aberdeen and Kincardine				X	X		X							
Angus	X	X		X	X		X	X	X		X		X	
Arygll and Bute					X			X	X					X
Ayr					X			X	X		X	X	X	X
Banff					X									
Berwick, Peebles, Roxburgh, Selkirk					X									
Caithness					X							X		
Clackmannan					X	X		X	X			X		
Dumfries		X		X	X	X	X	X	X					X
Dunbarton					X			X	X					
East and Mid Lothian					X									
Fife		X			X		X	X	X	X	X	X	X	
Inverness					X			X	X			X		
Kirkcudbright					X	X			X			X		X
Lanark														
Moray and Nairn					X	X	X							
Orkney and Zetland					X	X								
Perth and Kinross					X									
Renfrew					X			X	X			X	X	
Ross and Cromarty and Sutherland					X									
Stirling					X									
West Lothian					X			X						
Wigtown					X	X	X	X						X
Large Burghs														
Airdrie and Coatbridge					X									
Dumbarton and Clydebank					X									
Greenock	X	X	X	X	X									
Kilmarnock					X						X		X	
Paisley					X	X								
Perth					X			X				X	X	
Cities														
Aberdeen					X									X
Dundee					X			X						X
Edinburgh					X	X			X					
Glasgow		X			X			X	X				X	

Memorandum by the
Institute of Baths Management

The Structure, Administration and Effectiveness of Local Authorities

Preamble

1. In submitting this evidence the Institute has restricted its recommendations to matters which affect the administrative efficiency of local government in general, or the efficiency and future of the Baths Service in particular. The structural deficiencies of a service mainly of Victorian origin with far too many authorities administering fragmentary areas, with insignificant powers and inadequate financial resources, are so patently obvious as to need no comment.

ORGANISATION

Size of Local Councils

2. There is an inadequate supply of competent candidates in local elections. Lack of prestige of Council members is undoubtedly one of the reasons for disinterest. A substantial reduction in the size of Councils would both enhance members' prestige and reduce the demand for competent candidates to nearer the available supply.

Size of Committees

3. The effectiveness of Committees varies inversely to their size. Diminishment of Committee size from sixteen, seventeen, or eighteen members so frequently encountered in local authorities would undoubtedly increase efficiency. The extent of reduction should only be limited by the need to preserve democracy by ensuring adequate representation. Less than seven members might be considered too small but undoubtedly more than nine is too many.

4. A diminishment in Committee size would be a natural consequence of diminishment in the size of Councils. Individual members would have more time in which to express their views and more opportunity of attaining a Chairmanship. There would also be a proportionate reduction in the cost of stationery, postage and refundable expenses to members.

Frequency of Committee Meeting

5. The general fixed pattern of monthly meetings is completely incompatible with the immense variation in the size and functions of different departments. In many small departments officers are hard put to assemble adequate agenda and in consequence their Committees frequently descend to dealing with minor management problems. This diminishes the prestige of both the officers and their Committees.

6. Conversely, certain departments' agenda are so bulky that the time available is insufficient to permit adequate consideration. In some cases, authorities have been forced to institute more frequent meetings for such Committees, but the obvious corollary of bi-monthly or even quarterly meetings for certain smaller departments is rarely inaugurated.

Delegation of Powers to Committees

7. Failure of most Councils to exercise their statutory powers to confer full delegation on their Committees is probably the greatest single cause of operational inefficiency in local government. Submission of Committee resolutions for Council approval does not only impose delay in implementation. Written reports are expanded considerably to include information which could be imparted verbally at Committee meetings, in order to meet the eventuality of other Council members raising ill informed voices at the subsequent Council meeting. Frequently such expansion, which is costly in officers' time and stationery, defeats its own objectives by increasing the total volume of written matter to a point where it is only skimmed or not read at all.

8. Without full delegation, Committees function under the shadow of the Council. Lack of full responsibility feeds timidity, inhibits action and encourages deferment. Reports are referred to other Committees as a defence mechanism against possible future objection and the whole administrative machine snowballs into a morass of duplication and internal circulation of memoranda with all the inseparable attendant clerical costs and delays.

Demarcation between Managerial and Policy Functions

9. Councils' Standing Orders include terms of reference to Committees to avoid overlapping of functions and the consequent possibility of disputes. Unfortunately, this wise precaution is not extended to the powers of Committees and their Chief Officials. Frequently Committees become involved in minor management problems without any policy implications. This practice undermines the responsibility of departmental heads and introduces an aura of uncertainty and timidity into the operation of management. Conversely, with an undefined borderline between management and policy, officials cannot be sure on certain issues whether to act or refer.

10. Obviously on many issues there is an interpenetration of management and policy on which consultation with the Committee Chairman is advisable. There are a multitude of other issues, however, on which simple terms of reference could be formed. Examination of Committee procedures within a single authority usually reveals disparities in practice. Investigation of such anomalies frequently shows that the differences are not the result of conscious decisions by the Committees concerned, but have merely emanated in the first place from varying ideas of Chief Officials as to the extent of their powers. Provision of clear cut terms of reference on easily definable powers would eliminate uncertainty, promote uniformity of treatment and prevent some Committees wasting time on certain items which in another Committee of the same authority are dealt with directly by the department's chief officers. And to promote democratic efficiency the line of demarcation between management and policy functions should be as high as possible.

OPERATION

Control of Departments

11. Many small authorities and even some sizeable County Boroughs group certain departments under the control of Principal Officers. In the experience of the Institute where baths departments are administered in this way, they are almost invariably less progressive.

12. If efficient and enthusiastic officers are subjected to uninformed interference or have to channel their ideas through another officer with no real appreciation of their problems then they tend to become frustrated and to lose interest. If the control is purely nominal then they resent being the *de facto* manager without recognition and probably without

the appropriate remuneration. In either case, if young enough, they are likely to move to another and more enlightened authority. If too old to move, they might well lessen their efforts to effect improvements.

13. The fact that a department is small does not diminish the need for properly qualified management. Also the fact that a Principal Officer may be a highly qualified lawyer or engineer does not endow him with an understanding of the peculiar specialist knowledge required to manage a baths service or for that matter, a Parks, Cleansing, Libraries or Lighting Department, etc.

14. Any reform of local government must lead to the creation of larger authorities and consequently to an expansion of all departments. Elimination of the practice of grouping departments under blanket control would procure two desirable objectives

15. Firstly, Principal Officers would be relieved of extraneous responsibilities and enabled to devote all their energy to the administration of their enlarged departments. This point would be even more important in the event of the development of the City Manager system. Managerial efficiency demands quick decisions and it is vital that Departmental Managers should be in a position to give them and not become a link in a paper chain of reports, memoranda, requisitions and approvals flowing backwards and forwards to the City Manager and his staff with all the consequential delays and irritations.

16. Secondly, the reduction in the number of managerial promotion opportunities in the baths service would be partially offset by the elevation in salaries arising from increased responsibility and the greater attraction of independent responsibility. Any improvement in attraction of recruitment is most important. Modern swimming pools, because of the complexity of plant usually cost more than any other single public amenity, and because of the financial and public health aspects of competent control, it is essential to procure properly qualified managers. The baths service now stands on the threshold of a continuing period of rapid expansion which will increase the need to recruit officers of the right calibre. This will necessitate a substantial increase in both salaries and prestige. Salary levels will rise with scarcity but an immediate increase in prestige would result from the creation of independent responsibility wherever possible.

Duplication and Underuse of Amenities

17. The vertical structure of most Standing Committees has created a departmentalist attitude leading to the provision of facilities purely to serve departmental functions, despite the obvious capital and operating economies of dual use. In the baths service there are many instances of housing department laundries and public laundries competing in the same area for a diminishing trade.

18. The main example, however, is the development of school swimming pools. Well over 5,000 have been built since the war and the vast majority of them are only used between 9.00 a.m. and 4.00 p.m. on five days of the week, for less than nine months of the year. Except for very small initial teaching pools, all swimming pools should be designed to serve the whole community. On the Continent, it is not current practice to provide school pools as an integral part of school buildings. Usually they are sited adjacent to the school with direct enclosed access and a completely separate public entrance to the other side.

19. In view of the high capital cost of swimming pools and the fact that the Baths and Education services are both provided and operated by local authorities, it is nonsensical that duplication of this sort should be allowed. Continuation of this process can only lead to the ultimate stupidity of local authorities providing at immense capital cost, two sets of swimming pools; public buildings standing almost completely idle during school hours and school pools standing idle out of school hours.

20. All local authority services should be reviewed to ascertain functions which could be better performed by a single specialist department irrespective of departmental pre-serves. Consolidation should provide more efficient operation plus an overall reduction in the capital cost of provision and operation.

Control of School Pools

21. Institute Members are frequently called on for advice when school pool plants run into operating difficulties and are almost invariably appalled at the conditions revealed. Most school pools are operated by caretakers, boilermen or even gardeners with no knowledge of water treatment, chemical testing, or plant operation. Frequently the bacteriological conditions of the water in such pools is positively dangerous.

22. It is not always appreciated that indoor school pools are usually operated at higher temperatures than public pools, and that this accelerates the growth of pathogenic bacteria. Also there is a common fallacy that because daytime use is limited to successive school classes the pollution is less than in public pools which permits the installation of less adequate plant and the use of unskilled control. In fact the throughput of public pools divided into their far greater volumetric capacities of water frequently reveals that the hourly pollution per gallon in a school pool is far greater than in a public pool. Consequently an even higher standard of plant and control is needed in the case of a school pool than with a public pool.

23. These facts should be impressed on local education authorities and frequent regular inspections should be carried out by Health authorities to ensure that adequate standards of water treatment are maintained.

24. Many authorities, including most of the larger County Boroughs adopt the obvious solution of placing school pools under the technical control of their Baths Manager. Some authorities, however, have school pools but no public baths department. Also, many school baths are not under the control of local education authorities. The only answer to this dangerous and rapidly growing situation is to follow the example of some American health authorities in instituting a licensing system to ensure that only certificated operators are allowed to control swimming pool plants.

25. In view of the increasing hazard to public health and the repercussions on the public bath service of any epidemic traced to use of a swimming pool, the Institute is at present preparing a scheme for the certification of such employees.

Co-operation between adjacent Authorities

26. The use of swimming pools is not contained by local authority boundaries. The newly created Regional Sports Councils will prevent the building of International size baths where district size pools are adequate or the unreasonably close siting of pools provided by adjacent authorities. They do not appear, however, to have any power to inspire joint provision and the sharing of capital and operating costs.

27. Reconstruction of local government involving the creation of much larger areas will help solve this problem, but will take several years and in the meantime the advocacy and encouragement of joint provision which has emanated from the Minister of Housing and Local Government (e.g. Circular No. 31/66) could result in the earlier provision of desirable amenities in underprovided areas, if positive means of implementation were created. In this connection the statutory formation of Standing Joint Committees of neighbouring authorities would provide the vehicle for the transmission of ideas as to possible forms of co-operation. Such Committees would also provide the forum for prior consideration of the problems of amalgamation which must inevitably come about in the future.

FINANCE

Financial Regulations

28. The financial regulations of local authorities appear to be designed to stop misuse of a single penny of public money irrespective of the fact that it might cost £1 to do so.

29. It is of course highly desirable that probity of local government officials is above suspicion and that it shall be manifest to the general public that such is the case. It should not be difficult, however, to design a system which inhibits fraud but relieves officials from the cumbersome and sometimes quite useless current financial procedures. Possibly the most ridiculous example of financial control is the use of Requisition Books which, while they can be justified theoretically, are utterly useless in practice.

30. More important is the time and paper wasting procedure so often adopted of dual or even treble consideration of each expenditure proposal. Reports submitted at the proposed time of purchase on items which have been provided for in the Annual Financial Estimates merely duplicate the process of authorisation.

31. The process of preparation of annual estimates involves an immense amount of work and the way in which they progress towards obtaining Council sanction involves considerable waste of officers' and Committees' time. The usual procedure is commencement of preparation of estimates in September, October or November, followed by careful vetting by an officer of the City Treasurer's Department, and then submission for Committee approval. Frequently a Sub-Committee is delegated to examine the draft estimates and then their work is duplicated by consideration by the whole Committee. The next stage is submission to the Finance Committee, who inevitably return them to the departmental Committees to effect a reduction. Consideration by Sub-Committee and full Committee then follows, and after effecting reductions the estimates are re-submitted to the Finance Committee.

32. The whole procedure is designed to tailor the individual financial demands of the various Committees to fit a total budget which in the final analysis will be determined by the Finance Committee and the Council. How much simpler it would be if the Finance Committee received rough estimates of departmental expenditure and then decided the total budget. After Council approval of this total and with the size of the rate demand known, the various committees would be allocated their share. It would then be up to the Committees to frame their estimates to meet their allocation. All submission, re-submission, consideration and reconsideration by Committees, and discussions between Departmental and Treasurer's Officials would be dispensed with, together with all the special pleading and shadow boxing and the common practice of loading estimates to provide sacrificial cows for subsequent axing. This procedure would not only economise in time but would enhance the Committee's authority.

Capital Cost of Swimming Pools

33. The high capital cost of swimming pools is undoubtedly the reason for the extremely slow rate of progress in the provision of additional buildings and the retention in service of so many premises of Victorian origin, with totally inadequate comfort effects. The Institute can see no reason why the conditions of the Local Government Miscellaneous Provisions Act 1953 should not be altered to allow a local authority to save substantial sums annually towards the provision of particular amenities so that by the date of erection they will be entirely, or substantially, free from debt, thereby eliminating the millstone of annual debt charges, which have increased so greatly with the escalation of interest rates. It would also be advantageous to make the power of setting up renewals funds for replacement of plant mandatory which would help local authorities to replace plant at the end of its economic life. Similarly, the setting up of a renewals fund for the whole building, say over a 40 or 50 year term would encourage more frequent replacement of public amenities.

Scale of Provision

34. There are extremely wide differences in the scale of Baths and Public Laundry services provided by local authorities throughout the country, varying from the almost palatial to none at all.

35. The facilities offered do not, as they might be thought to, coincide with the type of authority. Some small but enlightened authorities provide a first class service whilst some larger towns offer a very low one or indeed none. Much has depended in the past upon the public spirit of the members of various Councils or the community feeling in particular towns. The effect of this has been a great unevenness with parts of the country well served and other areas poorly so.

36. Because of this the Institute considers that the time has not only arrived but is long overdue for minimum standards for the Baths service to be governed by statute as has been done in the case of public libraries by the Public Libraries and Museums Act 1964. In this connection the Institute would be pleased to offer any assistance possible in the appointment of a Working Party or in any other way.

FOOTNOTE

Definition of the Baths Service

The Existing Service

37. The Public Baths Service in the British Isles comprises indoor and open air swimming pools, hot bath suites, central laundries, establishment laundries, public laundries and Turkish, Russian, Aeratone, Sauna, and various other therapeutic bath amenities. A large number of indoor swimming pools are converted to public halls in the winter season and some baths departments administer permanent public halls. These halls are used for such functions as dancing, public meetings, socials, concerts, boxing, wrestling, bowls, tennis, cricket, badminton, table tennis, golf practice, judo, dinners, exhibitions, dog shows, cat shows, rabbit shows, roller skating, gymnastics, netball, basket ball, volleyball and various other purposes.

Existing Ancillary Services

38. Many baths departments use their central laundries to perform part or all of their authorities' laundering needs. Some baths departments control their authorities' public conveniencies. Some are responsible for the maintenance of other buildings and boiler plants. A number use boiler plants in their baths establishments to provide heat for adjacent Council Buildings. Seaside baths departments frequently control foreshore amenities. And a few baths departments administer most other forms of local-authority provided recreations and entertainments in their areas.

Future Services

39. The economic advantages of integrating permanent recreational amenities in a single building and the current widespread interest in recreation inspired by the Sports Council has led to the submission to the Regional Sports Councils of a large number of schemes for the provision of multi purpose sports and recreation complexes based on swimming pools and their ancillaries. It is evident therefore that the Baths Service of the future will move closer towards the provision of recreation in general and away from its traditional but dying functions of providing public laundering and private bath facilities.

Memorandum by the
British Veterinary Association, Scottish Branch

1. Scottish Branch of the British Veterinary Association wish to present the following memorandum as evidence to the above Royal Commission in relation to provision of slaughterhouse facilities.

2. There is a trend for the older slaughterhouses which cannot comply with the regulations to be closed down by the local authorities. Since many of these buildings are of approximately the same age and are in some cases in neighbouring communities, whole areas may be deprived of facilities. The provision of abattoir facilities is the responsibility of the local authorities and the only likely replacements, under the current regulations, would be the building of new small establishments and this is already taking place. This process is both uneconomic, when one considers the small numbers of animals likely to be handled at each unit, and unwise, since it would impede development. The provision of large slaughterhouses sited strategically so that they could serve a sizeable area, would afford the opportunity of establishing units with up to date facilities for ante-mortem and post-mortem examinations. This concept would be economically desirable, would be large enough to justify full-time veterinary supervision with subsequent benefit to public health and would favour the development of a uniform system of inspection and definite standards.

3. It is also felt that due consideration should be given to the requirements of the European Economic Community in the field of slaughterhouses and meat inspection and that all future developments should be capable of fitting in with these requirements. Only a few of the present larger slaughterhouses could meet these requirements at the moment.

4. With regard to meat inspection we are aware of the recommendations of the Verdon-Smith Committee (Command 2282) but note from the subsequent White Paper (Command 2737) that it is the Government's intention to set up a meat and livestock commission whose terms of reference will only in part implement the recommendations of the Verdon-Smith Committee. We note in particular that: "the commission would not, however, be charged with the responsibility for hygienic standards in slaughterhouses nor for meat inspection. These are matters touching upon public health, which, in the Government's view, should remain under public control".

5. We presume that this later point does not rule out a nationally organised meat inspection service which could of course be representative of the local authorities.

6. We recommend therefore that meat inspection, licensing of slaughterhouses and all matters concerning slaughterhouses should be the concern of a central authority and not of the local authorities. We suggest that slaughterhouses should be sufficiently large wherever possible to employ a full-time veterinary specialist in this field. It is recognised that the suggested central authority is largely dependent on national decisions, so in the event of this recommendation being unacceptable, we suggest that wherever possible smaller local authorities should combine to administer these large regional slaughterhouses and that the veterinary surgeon in charge should also be responsible for the duties set out in paragraph 7. Large local authorities could of course implement these recommendations with their present resources.

7. We recommend that it would be in the public interest to appoint veterinary surgeons to organise the professional functions which are the responsibility of local authorities in connection with the following: The Diseases of Animals Act 1950 and orders following thereon, which include the supervision of markets and transport of livestock; the Pro-

tection of Animals (Scotland) Act 1912; the Riding Establishments Act 1964; the Animals Boarding Establishments Act 1963; the Pet Animals Act 1951; veterinary duties under the Milk and Dairies (Scotland) Act 1914; and in duties concerning the preparation and distribution of meat.

8. To make for more efficient working and for uniformity throughout the country all Inspectors appointed by the local authority under the Diseases of Animals Act 1950 should be Police Officers.

9. Finally, we feel that the number of officers who have the power to enter dairies for various purposes is unreasonably large and in our opinion efforts should be made to co-ordinate and reduce this number with resultant economy and increased efficiency.

Memorandum by the
Association of River Inspectors of Scotland

1. This memorandum is divided into two main parts, viz:—

   (a) consideration of the possible reorganisation of existing local government authorities with respect to their functions of drainage, sewage purification (including acceptance and treatment of industrial discharges), water abstraction and aspects of their responsibilities which may affect rivers in any way; and

   (b) the role of River Purification Boards themselves.

LOCAL GOVERNMENT AUTHORITIES

2. As at present constituted these authorities vary very considerably in size through counties, cities down to a wide range of burghs. Their boundaries bear no relationship to natural drainage areas. Some are so large that they are unwieldy for the functions under consideration; others so small that they have difficulty in providing the necessary equipment and particularly the specialist trained personnel to carry out those functions. In some authorities, particularly though not exclusively the smaller ones, some of the officers have so many duties that they cannot be expert in them all.

3. Drainage, sewage purification and water pollution control have little popular appeal or vote-catching power unless and until something is obviously and grossly wrong—and not always then, if the more serious consequences occur outside the boundaries of the authority responsible. The allocation of funds or of officials' time and attention to such matters is liable to suffer in competition with other more spectacular functions of local government.

Recommendations

4. We recommend that:—

   (a) Single-purpose authorities should be formed for the drainage and treatment of waste waters, both domestic and, where appropriate, industrial.

   (b) Their boundaries should be based on areas of natural physical geography or a group of such areas and would not necessarily coincide with those for other local government purposes, such as education, housing, police, etc.

   (c) Their governing body should be a Board consisting of representatives of constituent local authorities (dependent on the ultimate structure of local government in general) and members appointed by the Secretary of State for Scotland to represent industry and other specific interests.

   (d) The administration of each such authority should be by a technical manager holding such qualifications as the Secretary of State for Scotland may by Order prescribe.

   (e) The financing of such a Board will depend on the ultimate arrangements for local government as a whole, but might be by precept on constituent authorities, by local tax levied on individuals and industry in the area or by an allocation from central funds. The final decision as to finance should not affect our other recommendations.

   (f) A suitable model for the type of authority we have in mind may be found in the Upper Tame Drainage Authority in the Birmingham area.

RIVER PURIFICATION BOARDS

5. The present areas of River Purification Boards are in accordance with natural physical geography. They consist of either a single river catchment area or a group of adjacent ones. These areas have proved generally satisfactory in practice, though some adjustments may be desirable.

6. An anomaly exists in southern Scotland because the River Purification Board boundaries follow the national boundary, whereas the natural catchments of the Tweed and Border Esk lie both sides of the border between England and Scotland. The effect is accentuated by the different statutory functions of river authorities on each side of the Border, referred to below in paragraphs 10 and 11.

7. North of the Caledonian Canal and in a few areas south of it, pollution prevention legislation is administered by the County Councils acting as river purification authorities. This was not unreasonable having regard to the distribution of population and industry and to the consequent pollution potential. However any considerable intensification of industry and therefore of population in parts of this area renders reconsideration of the position necessary. Moreover any reorganisation of local government for this zone should take account of what is to happen to the river purification function there.

8. One of the principal reasons for the formation of River Boards in England following the 1948 Act and of River Purification Boards in Scotland by the 1951 Act was that previous pollution prevention legislation had been administered by local authorities, who were in many cases themselves the worst potential offenders. Hence it was thought best to set up independent Boards to administer the law, having regard to the management of a river as a whole unit. It would be very unfortunate if any reorganisation of local government reverted to the previous position whereby the same authority had a dual and opposing interest, which could lead to a clash.

9. This position still arises to a limited extent where a River Purification Board has substantially the same boundaries as a single County Council, one of whose principal officers serves the River Purification Board in a part-time capacity and whose members form a majority of that Board.

10. Differences in the law relating to the functions of river authorities and to the acceptance of trade wastes into local authority sewers exist in Scotland as compared with England and Wales. These matters may not come within the terms of reference of this Royal Commission but we mention them in case they do. They materially affect the object of the inquiry and should be considered as at least relevant to it.

11. The functions of river authorities in England and Wales cover a wider field than those of river purification authorities in Scotland. They include practical engineering duties (such as flood prevention, river straightening, dredging, weed-cutting and works to regulate flow), management of fisheries and comprehensive management of the water resources of their areas as well as the Scottish functions of river flow gauging and the administration of legislation for river pollution prevention.

12. In the Ruhr region of West Germany equivalent organisations exercise still more complete control over every aspect of river management. They design and construct impounding reservoirs to regulate the downstream flow for all purposes, including in some cases the supply of water to underground strata in order to augment wells. Incidentally where dams are built for the above purposes, the outflow is often used to generate hydro-electricity in stations built and operated by the same organisations. They exercise all the functions of British river authorities. The most important addition is that the same boards in Germany also design, construct, operate and maintain sewage treatment plants, dealing with mixed domestic and trade wastes, and some for special industrial liquors alone. This practice may appear to run counter to the argument (in paragraph 8 above) against

the same authority simultaneously producing a discharge and prescribing the standard of quality the discharge should achieve. To some extent this is so; but there is the important difference that in Germany the producing body is a specialist one, concentrating solely on and fully conversant with every facet of the regimen of the whole river, whereas in Britain it was a general-purpose local authority with a very narrow interest in only a limited stretch of river and to whom sewage purification was often of very sub-ordinate consideration.

13. The structure of River Purification Boards, with representatives of local authorities and Secretary of State nominees, has proved very practicable and practical. It serves as the basis for our recommendation 4(c) for single-purpose authorities in general. In a few instances Boards could usefully be smaller in numerical size.

Recommendations

14. We recommend that:—

    (a) River Purification Boards should remain independent river management authorities with boundaries based on geographical watersheds.

    (b) Some adjustment of their boundaries should be considered in the light of experience and particular consideration given to those boundaries which at present abut the Border with England.

    (c) Consideration should be given to possible extensions of the functions of River Purification Boards, in the light of both the English and German systems. We do not necessarily advocate the adoption of either scheme in full, but suggest that both should be studied closely with a view to legislating for such parts as may best suit Scottish conditions.

Memorandum by the
Institute of Burial and Cremation Administration

Present circumstances

1. In the modern conditions small segregated units of local government almost invariably are unable to provide the efficient operation of small burial grounds owing to the burden on available funds and the consequential inability to employ good quality staff. The acquisition of mechanical aids to overcome deficiencies in the labour force is expensive and cannot always be fully employed in a small burial ground. The lack of opportunities in small burial authorities for qualified staff, administrative and manual, with commensurate rates of pay makes such work unattractive as a career and so militates against efficient operation.

2. The tendency in recent years to overcome financial and staffing difficulties by incorporating burial and cremation administration in a larger department whose main duties bear little or no relation to the function of disposing of the dead, is liable to produce at top level an indifferent attitude towards this administration which the burial and cremation staff and the bereaved public naturally resent. Such conditions are not normally conducive to fullest economy and efficiency in working arrangements.

Suggestions for reform

3. The central control of the disposal of the dead should be exercised at County or City level by a Standing Committee responsible solely for this part of public service, and the administration divided into districts that will provide the maximum efficiency in local burial arrangements and burial ground maintenance. Small burial grounds could then be grouped for efficient working with qualified staff and the most effective mechanical aids which for economic reasons could not be provided independently by small authorities.

4. The Chief Officer of the Standing Committee should be fully qualified and well experienced in burial and cremation administration, and each district managed by a similarly qualified and experienced officer. This would avoid the danger of remote control which is against the public interest in a service about which the public are so highly sensitive, and establish some measure of personal interest in the administration at local level which the public expect.

5. Where there is a crematorium or need for a crematorium in the County or City area, it should be sited, managed and administered, as suggested for a district in the burial administration.

6. The foregoing arrangement would spread the financial burden of providing the necessary efficiency in staffing and mechanisation, and would provide the opportunity of encouraging recruitment to the service as a career which is lacking so much in the present administrative arrangements to the detriment of a vital service which is of some importance in the maintenance of public health and morale.

7. The appended Memorandum of the Institute on the Amalgamation of Areas of Local Government was prepared for consideration in England and Wales, but it is submitted herewith as much of its contents is relevant in the present inquiry into local government arrangements in Scotland.

October, 1966.

Appendix

The Amalgamation of Areas of Local Government as it may concern the Administration of Cemeteries and Crematoria

1. This Institute recognises the need for the reorganisation of local government areas and understands that the formation of new and larger authorities is designed to provide for the ratepayer a greater efficiency of all the existing services at the lowest possible cost. The amalgamation of Cemetery and Crematorium services with other departments does not create greater efficiency or reduce cost. Larger Cemetery and Crematorium Departments formed by an aggregation of authorities would, however, make for more efficient administration.

2. The Institute acknowledges that it would be unrealistic to assume that the absorption of existing authorities with long established and cherished habits of administration, into the new concentrations, can be achieved without considerable stress and strain to both members and officers. It is firmly of the opinion, however, that these problems can best be resolved by retaining a clear picture of the purpose of the new authorities, namely that they shall provide the ratepayer with a more efficient service. With this in mind, the Institute is greatly concerned that with the formation of larger departments, the control of the essential service to the public of the Disposal of the Dead will become remote and impersonal. There is no period in a person's life other than at the time of bereavement, when it is more essential for personal and sympathetic service to be given and for the officers who are responsible for the management in this most important field of public relationship to be readily available.

3. The Institute reiterates that this section of local government is of so unique a character that it requires always to be organised as a special department. It is a viable entity which is best able to perform its specialised functions within its own particular environment. It is conceded that some small authorities have found it necessary that the Cemetery or Crematorium should be related to one of the other departments for the purpose of administration, but with the genesis of the new larger authorities, it is highly desirable that the Cemeteries and Crematoria should be administered by an autonomous department and be the concern of a separate committee or sub-committee. If, however, it is deemed unavoidable for this service to be related to one of the main departments of a local authority, the requirements of the service indicate that its natural adherence should be to the Town Clerk or the Medical Officer.

4. This Institute, therefore, urges with all the force at its command, that in the setting up of the newly constituted authorities, this Memorandum of the Institute, expressing the considered opinion of officers most able to judge the merits of the aggregation of the services for the Disposal of the Dead, shall receive the most careful consideration.

5. The Institute of Burial and Cremation Administration was established in 1913, with the objects of promoting and improving Cemeteries and Crematoria by fostering a fuller knowledge of the work required for their management and administration and thereby creating an efficient public service for the Disposal of the Dead. It is the only organisation of administrative officers which deals exclusively and comprehensively with this public service.

6. The Institute meets in conference annually, combining with the Organisation for the employing authorities, the Federation of British Cremation Authorities. Through a governing Council and eight Branches, it works generally to improve and develop the technical and general knowledge and efficiency of persons employed in the administration

of Cemeteries and Crematoria throughout Great Britain. It provides educational facilities, holds examinations and grants diplomas and certificates of proficiency, which ensures that qualified members are proficient in such varied subjects as Burial and Cremation Law, Administration and Management of Cemeteries and Crematoria, Layout of Cemeteries and Gardens of Remembrance, and Horticulture.

7. Superintendents and Registrars of Cemeteries and Crematoria who are members of the Institute have always been aware of their responsibilities to administer this service with dignity and efficiency and do take this opportunity to affirm that, as responsible members of this professional Institute, they look forward to the new challenge presented by the reorganisation of areas, in the expectation that it will provide them with greater scope for the exercise of their specialised skill, experience and expert knowledge.

Memorandum by the
Association of Registrars of Scotland

1. The particular aspect of the local government service in Scotland with which the Association of Registrars of Scotland is directly concerned relates to the duties laid upon local authorities by the Registration of Births, Deaths and Marriages (Scotland) Act, 1965. (hereinafter referred to as the 1965 Act).

2. Under the terms of this Act, each local authority which, prior to the commencement of the 1965 Act, had registration functions (i.e. large burghs, counties and cities) is a local registration authority, and the area of a local registration authority consists of the area embracing all the registration districts for which the local registration authority is responsible.

Responsibility for the Registration Service in Scotland

3. The 1965 Act divided responsibility for the administration of the registration service in Scotland between the local registration authority and the Registrar General, and, in broad terms, the responsibilities are shared as follows.

The Local Registration Authority

4. Subject to consultation with the Registrar General, may prepare schemes for the purpose of altering the number, boundaries or titles of the registration districts within its area. Such schemes must be submitted to the Secretary of State for his approval after due public intimation and, if he thinks fit, a local enquiry has been held.

5. Subject to certain provisions, appoints registrars of births, deaths and marriages (district registrars) and may appoint—

(a) additional district registrars

(b) senior registrars

(c) assistant registrars

6. In the case of 5(a) and (b) the appointment may be made only after consultation with the Registrar General.

7. Persons appointed under 5 above are deemed to be employees of the local registration authority.

8. Subject to certain conditions of age and superannuation regulations, may remove from offices those appointed as in 5 above.

9. When necessary, may appoint an *interim* registrar, but should it fail to do so when such an appointment is necessary, the Registrar General or the Secretary of State at the request of the Registrar General may require it so to do.

10. Provide adequate staff for registration offices within its area.

11. After consultation with the Registrar General, determine the salaries of the registration staff.

12. May be required, by regulations made by the Secretary of State, to pay compensation to or in respect of any person who suffers loss of employment or diminution of office.

13. Provide and maintain a suitable office for each registration district, and defray the running costs thereof.

14. Cause a notice board to be displayed on or near the registration office and fix the hours of attendance.

15. Have custody of the duplicate office keys and duplicate safe keys.

16. Where circumstances justify, and with the approval of the Registrar General, provide and maintain a suitable area repository in which registers may be stored.

17. Receive fees collected by registrars in the execution of their duties.

The Registrar General

18. Has power "to do all such things as appear to him necessary or expedient for maintaining the utility and efficiency of the registration service in Scotland". This covers all matters dealing with registration practice and procedure.

Comparison of Duties

19. A comparison of the division of duties between the local registration authority and the Registrar General shows:—

(a) the local registration authority is mainly concerned with making staff appointments, cost of maintaining the service and provision of accommodation.

(b) in most of the duties of the local registration authority, approval consultation or authority is required from the Registrar General and/or the Secretary of State before the authority may act.

(c) the Registrar General's interest covers every aspect of the actual process of registration. He alone issues instructions to registration staff, and any consultation on specific registration matters is between the registrar and the Registrar General and never with the local registration authority.

Control of the Registration Service

20. The present dual control of the registration service is detrimental to its efficiency.

21. The service is clearly a national one, centrally controlled in all its aspects in so far as actual registration procedure is concerned. On the other hand, it is locally organised and maintained. Thus the Registrar General, who is bound to require a certain standard of efficiency and service, is not in a position to ensure that such standard is always provided.

22. The local nature of the organisation of the service is such that considerable disparity exists in the conditions of employment between one authority and another. This causes dissatisfaction among staff with a consequent adverse effect on the quality of the service rendered.

23. The fact that registration staff is deemed to be in the employment of the local registration authority, whereas the staff of the General Register Office is part of the civil service means that there can be no transfer of personnel from the central office to the local office or vice versa. Thus, the considerable experience in the field of many registrars and assistant registrars is lost to the central office and vice versa.

24. Further evidence of the national aspect of the registration service is borne out by the fact that no longer is it only local events which are recorded in a local registration office. In fact the births and deaths recorded may have occurred in any other locality in Scotland, and in the case of marriages, the choice of place of marriage (particularly in

the case of civil marriages) is not necessarily governed by the locality of residence. Thus, a local registration authority is often providing a service which is in fact serving a very much wider area than its own.

Proposal

25. The Association of Registrars of Scotland considers that there is an unanswerable case for the central control of the registration service as a whole because:—

    (*a*) the service is clearly national rather than local.

    (*b*) the local registration authority has no real control or interest in the service.

and   (*c*) by abolishing the existing division of responsibility and placing the registration service under the sole control of a central department, the efficient administration of the service would be enhanced and a better service to the public provided.

26. The Association suggests therefore that the registration service should be taken outwith the function of local government and the entire responsibility for it should be assumed by central government through the Registrar General for Scotland.

27. The method whereby the transfer of the registration service would be achieved, requires fuller consideration than is possible in this memorandum. However, it might be on the lines of a complete transfer of the larger registration districts to the Registrar General's department and a system of agencies or similar arrangement in respect of the smaller registration districts.

28. If desired, the Association of Registrars of Scotland would be prepared to consider and submit suggestions as to how a transfer of the registration service to central control could be achieved.

Memorandum by the
Scottish Central Library

1. With reference to the invitation to submit evidence to the Royal Commission, my Executive Committee decided that it would be inappropriate for them to make any proposals regarding the general structure of Local Government in Scotland, or to offer suggestions for reform.

2. But I was directed to bring to your notice the precarious and unsatisfactory basis of the present arrangements for financial contributions to the Library by Scottish local authorities. This was summarised by a lecturer in the University of Strathclyde who said at a recent library conference:—

> "The first task then must be to place S.C.L. on a more secure financial basis. At present the vast bulk of its funds comes from the Treasury and local authorities in equal proportions (except in emergencies) thus greater self help would ensure greater government aid. There is need too to reform the machinery by which the contributions of individual libraries are assessed. The amount to be paid in each case is decided by the three local authority organisations. In the case of the counties and burghs this becomes mandatory when agreed to by a simple majority of the members, but only becomes mandatory on the cities where there is unanimous agreement. Thus any one of the cities can refuse to pay its share. Obviously unanimity has not been reached."

3. The Statute governing local authority contributions to the Scottish Central Library is the Public Libraries (Scotland) Act, 1955, and the relevant passage is Section 2.

4. The Scottish Central Library depends on Scottish Local Authorities for 50% of its income, the other 50% being provided by H.M. Government, through the Scottish Education Department.

5. In 1966, the Library was placed in serious financial straits arising out of the situation in which (1) the Association of County Councils (2) the Convention of Royal Burghs and (3) the Counties of Cities Association except for the City of Glasgow, all agreed to proposals for financing the Library.

6. My Executive Committee, and many independent observers, consider it wrong that any one of the four Cities should in this way be able to veto the express wishes of the other Cities, and the Counties and the Burghs.

7. My Executive Committee therefore hopes that the Royal Commission will take this matter into consideration when it formulates its conclusions.

M. C. Pottinger,
LIBRARIAN,
January, 1967.

Memorandum by the
Scottish Library Association

1. In the considered view of the Council of the Scottish Library Association, the public library service in Scotland suffers from the following defects which have seriously retarded its growth and full expansion:—

   (a) Many small library authorities have inadequate financial resources to maintain a sufficiently large book stock and to provide the qualified staff necessary for a fully effective service.

   (b) No official standards of efficiency have been adopted as a guide to library authorities in Scotland, such as are now in force in England.

   (c) No legal obligation exists in Scotland for library authorities to provide an effective service. As a result, there are wide variations in standards of library provision throughout the country.

   (d) Except in the cities, the library service in Scotland operates under two different acts of Parliament—the Public Libraries Acts in burghs, the Education (Scotland) Act in Counties.

   (e) As a result, there is considerable overlapping of services, with two libraries often operating in close proximity in the same town.

   (f) Arising from this unsatisfactory legal position, the anomaly of double rating for library services remains, and although satisfactory arrangements have been negotiated in some areas for compensatory payments by Counties to Burghs, resentment persists in other cases.

   (g) Certain limitations exist under the Public Libraries Acts which hinder expansion of the library service in such spheres as lectures, lending of gramophone records, pictures, etc.

   (h) The continued linking of Public Libraries and Museums under the same Act of Parliament tends to hinder the development of one or other of these services.

   (i) The arrangements for financing the Scottish Central Library under the Public Libraries (Scotland) Act, 1955, have caused considerable difficulty in the smooth functioning of the interlending service.

2. It is the submission of the Council that these defects could be remedied by the following reforms:—

   (a) Local authority areas should be re-grouped to ensure that each unit is large enough and financially viable to discharge its functions in an efficient manner according to modern standards of service.

   (b) So far as the public library service is concerned, we would regard a population figure of at least 100,000 as desirable to meet this requirement. It is recognised however that in the more sparsely populated areas of Scotland special problems exist, both financial and geographical, which make this impracticable.

   (c) As far as practicable, the grouping of local authority areas should contrive to link together for administrative purposes the rural areas surrounding towns, and to encourage the amalgamation of adjacent townships.

   (d) Every public library authority should have a statutory duty to provide an efficient library service, based on official standards to be adopted by the Secretary of State for Scotland, on the lines of those now in force for libraries in England and Wales.

(*e*) The Secretary of State should exercise a general responsibility for the oversight of the public library service, and should appoint an advisory body to assist him in this function.

(*f*) All public libraries should operate under one Public Libraries Act for Scotland, and a new Act should be passed to give effect to the changes outlined in this memorandum, and to consolidate and revise existing legislation affecting Scottish Public Libraries.

(*g*) Powers should be granted to library authorities to

(1) provide lectures, pay fees to lecturers, spend money on activities of a cultural nature and charge for admission to meetings or other functions.

(2) provide and lend such materials as gramophone records, pictures and films.

(3) acquire land compulsorily for library purposes.

(*h*) In the interests of readers using libraries outside their own areas, extra-district charges should be abolished, and any financial adjustment should be made by payment between library authorities themselves.

(*i*) The financial stability of the Scottish Central Library should be assured by amendment of the Public Libraries (Scotland) Act, 1955, or by some other means.

(*j*) Consideration should be given to separate legislative provision for Museums and Art Galleries.

(*k*) The public libraries service should remain free of any charge for the borrowing of books.

(*l*) A fully adequate public library service should include effective provision of books in hospitals, prisons, and similar institutions, and a home lending service for the old and disabled.

October, 1966.

Memorandum by the
Council for Museums and Galleries in Scotland

1. The Council was formed in 1964 and is composed of members representing over forty museum and art gallery-owning authorities in Scotland, including Universities and private bodies.

2. Its main purposes are:—

   (a) To promote interest in, encourage support for and organise measures aimed at extending the influence of, museums and galleries in Scotland as cultural, educational, recreational and social instruments.

   (b) To co-operate with authorities responsible for museums and galleries in the initiation and management of schemes designed to improve on existing standards of exhibitions, circulating displays and other museum and gallery services.

3. In subsequent paragraphs the word "museums" covers museums, art galleries and, where appropriate, art centres. A description of the functions and activities of museums is contained in an Appendix.

Museums in Scotland

4. Most of the museums in Scotland had their origin in the activities of individuals and local groups of people who were interested in collecting and preserving material which illustrated man's environment. The successful development of local museums throughout the years has been due to the devoted services given by these people and their museum officials. Not only have they interested themselves in the traditional work of museums, but also in the newer activities associated with these institutions. It is important that this local interest should be preserved.

5. Museums, however, have not yet achieved optimum influence, mainly because, through lack of public appreciation, resources have not been forthcoming or have not been made available. This lack of financial support, at least outside the four cities, has resulted in a shortage of skilled staff, insufficient supporting services and inadequate accommodation. These deficiencies have militated against the operation nationally of a fully developed museums service and should be remedied.

6. With this object in view the Council is co-operating with, and making available to, the smaller museums in Scotland, both public and private, advice and technical help which they cannot afford to provide themselves. The Council is giving the maximum possible help from its available resources.

Museums within a new Local Government Structure

7. In this context the Council has considered how the museums service can be improved in a changed local government system in Scotland.

8. Museum activities are "educational" in the broadest sense of that word. They are parallel to library and other cultural activities in the spheres of art, drama and music. All of them, with school and further education, on a formal and informal basis, comprise an area where there should be close association.

9. The connection between museums and formal school education is exemplified by the increasing use made by education authorities of school loans and other services. Many of the activities mentioned in the Appendix come within the category of further education.

10. Until the new Universities and Colleges have formed their own museums, and even afterwards, they will have to depend on existing museums for teaching purposes. In the developing field of educational television programmes, much use will be made of material available within museums.

11. The Council visualises, therefore, that museums should form part of a newly organised educational pattern coming within a single department of the major units of local government outlined in the White Paper Cmnd. 2067 "The Modernisation of Local Government in Scotland". This pattern would comprise the following services, but each would maintain a high degree of independence.

    (a) Education Services

        Formal school education

        Formal further education—technical colleges

        Informal further education—adult, etc.

        Television programmes

    (b) Libraries

    (c) Museums

    (d) Art, drama, music and other cultural services.

12. If the new units of local government are larger and regional, the Council would expect that greater resources would become available for the development of the museums service, and these resources could be used to better advantage. Instead of having a number of museums inadequately staffed, all the museums in the area could have the benefit of regional staff of varied skills, and a better distribution and exchange of exhibition material could be achieved. It would also follow that where a full museums service could not be justified in small localities, exhibition centres could be provided and staffed adequately.

13. In the event of a co-ordinated regional museum system being established, there would no longer exist the possibility of small localities attempting, without hope of success, to set up full museum services. Instead, and in order to encourage public interest in the preservation and display of suitable material, local exhibition centres would be provided and staffed on a co-operative basis.

Recommendations

14. The valuable local interest in museums should be retained, e.g. by having local museum advisory committees with specific remits and powers operating under the regional authorities which would be responsible for the service.

15. Since expansion of the museums service has been difficult because of the restricted resources of the present smaller local government units, museums in the future should be grouped in larger regions, and should be associated with other educational services in the region.

16. The museums service should be regarded as parallel to, but entirely separate from the Library Service for both administration and finance.

17. Under a regional system, the new authority as administrators of the museums service should be empowered to encourage and support financially and otherwise the private museums in their areas.

18. Any new authority, administering a large area or region, should be able to appoint qualified staff to serve on a joint basis, smaller museums which at present, because of financial limitations, are deprived of qualified staff.

19. While it is possible that the main City Museums will operate as Regional Museum Centres for their regions, new Regional Authorities should be eligible to become members of the Council and to subscribe to its funds.

20. The Council has various plans to bring museums more prominently before the public, and it would be glad to supplement the foregoing information in any way that might be required by the Royal Commission.

JAMES PIRIE GLEN
Chairman.

GEORGE A. YOUNG
Secretary.

APPENDIX

Functions and Activities of Museums

1. Museums are no longer solely the repositories of the dead past, but are today lively centres of widely varied activities. Sir Henry Miers reporting to the Carnegie United Kingdom Trustees in 1928 on the Public Museums of the British Isles restricted his report to museums, excluding art galleries from the scope of his report. Ten years later S. F. Markham reported to the same Trustees, but on the Museums and Art Galleries of the British Isles. In 1963, however, the members of the Standing Commission on Museums and Galleries are able to say in their Survey of Provincial Museums and Galleries (p. 34) that "It is not too much to say that the main museum of a town, quite apart from the educational part it should play in association with the local education authority, ought .... to be the centre of the artistic and intellectual life of the town."

2. One museum, for example, has in addition to its permanent museum and art collections, and loan exhibitions, the following activities: concerts, lectures, films, art appreciation group, and a lively Junior Museum Club. It also gives accommodation to art groups' and photographic exhibitions, naturalists, an aquarium society, astronomers, choral groups and a gramophone club. It has also an extensive schools loan service. A number of other museums in Scotland provide similar services as their contribution to the cultural and educational activities in their respective areas.

The Development of the Museums Service by the Council

3. In order that more effective use can be made of museums and their collections, the Council is encouraging the development of their services in a variety of ways. In the case of smaller museums the main provision is by way of advice and practical assistance, both professional and technical. This, however, is limited by the lack of financial resources available to the subscribing museums themselves and consequently to the Council.

4. The Council derives its income annually from subscriptions by museum owning authorities and other local sources and from a Treasury grant paid through the Scottish Education Department. The latter contribution amounts to 50% of the Council's gross annual expenditure. This means in effect, that the Treasury is prepared to contribute, within certain broad limits, up to the amount that the Council can raise from other sources. Local authorities, which form the main source, contribute in the case of Counties of Cities 10/- per thousand of population and in the case of burghs £1 per thousand of population. The former class of subscriber does not benefit directly from the professional and technical services provided by the Council. hence the lower rate of subscription.

5. The Education Authorities do not subscribe at present to the Council but it is hoped that, with the institution of circulating exhibition services among schools, support will be forthcoming from these authorities. Since museums are situated haphazardly in relation to existing authority boundaries and will be so in relation to new ones it would obviously be to the advantage of the museums service as a whole if it were to be financed from Educational funds on a regional basis.

6. The Council itself would find it helpful to deal financially with a limited number of Regional Authorities while preserving service links with museums on a local basis. Indeed, in the Council's view the money required for the proper development of museums and of the museums service is more likely to come from larger units of local government as visualised in the White Paper, Cmnd. 2067 " The Modernisation of Local Government in Scotland".

Memorandum by the
Scottish Federation of Museums and Art Galleries

1. The Scottish Federation of Museums and Art Galleries was formed in 1937 to bring together the professional men and women working in the museum service and the local authorities and other bodies responsible for museums and art galleries. Its aims are to promote close co-operation among the directors of museums and art galleries in the country, and the general advancement of the institutions in their care.

2. The Scottish Federation is affiliated to the Museums Association and many of its members also serve on the Council for Museums and Galleries in Scotland, which was formed through the efforts of the Federation.

3. In Scotland museums and art galleries fall into the following main categories:—

   (a) National Museums and Art Galleries;
   (b) Local Authority under the Counties of Cities (Aberdeen, Dundee, Edinburgh, Glasgow), various Burghs and County Councils;
   (c) University Museums;
   (d) Private Museums.

All of these have representation on the Scottish Federation.

4. While the larger institutions, especially in the cities, are administered by Museums and Art Galleries Committees many of the smaller museums are under the authority of Library Committees and librarians. Some of the private museums are governed by private trusts and, in spite of considerable efforts by the trustees, naturally suffer from the lack of qualified staff and finance and their future is uncertain. Many do not improve the public image of museums, their value in education and the other services museums can provide.

5. In a number of authorities the committee responsible for the museum is an *ad hoc* committee consisting of elected representatives and household members. In other instances persons with special knowledge or experience are co-opted to the committee. This would appear to be a satisfactory system in relation to museums and art galleries.

6. In relation to the future development of museum and art gallery services we would refer the Royal Commission to the "Survey of Provincial Museums and Galleries" carried out by the Standing Commission on Museums and Galleries and published by H.M.S.O. in 1963. This survey recommended among other things better display and staffing, the extension of educational services, capital assistance towards buildings and increased funds for purchases.

Recommendations

7. While it is naturally impossible to foresee the future structure of Local Government in Scotland we submit that much of the museum service would benefit if based on larger units of administration.

8. We also recommend that:—

   (a) The museum service, while perhaps not being an integral part of, should be closely associated with the educational services for all age groups.
   (b) That greater use should be made by the educational services of the facilities already provided by some museums and that these facilities should be extended

to cover larger areas. This would necessitate providing more adequate funds and suitably qualified staff for museums which are at present administered by small local authorities.

(c) That the formation of a system of larger administrative areas would encourage smaller museum-owning authorities to combine to provide professionally qualified curatorial staff to serve, on a joint basis, two or more museums in adjacent localities.

(d) While it is recognised that association between library and museum services can, in certain instances, be advantageous, under any new local government structure museum services should be separated from library services for administration and finance. Each museum, or group of museums, should have a professionally qualified museum director responsible to a Museum and Art Gallery Committee, which in turn would be directly responsible to the local Council.

(e) The present practice, in many authorities, of having co-opted members on their museum committees should be continued and provision made for these authorities to co-opt suitable persons with knowledge of and interest in museum work.

(f) Provision should be made for local authorities, in particular the larger authorities, to provide financial and other support to private museums in their areas and to enter into legal agreements to safeguard the future of the collections in these museums.

(g) While it is realised that it may not be of direct concern within the reorganisation of local government to provide capital for buildings, every encouragement should be given for the setting up of a scheme for capital assistance as recommended by the Standing Commission. This grant system should utilise the channel already existing through the Standing Commission and the Council for Museums and Galleries in Scotland. The present capital grants system through the Arts Council does not aid the provision of premises for permanent museum collections, but only for buildings to house such things as temporary exhibitions and lecture halls.

(h) That local authorities should be encouraged to develop the educational potential of their local art galleries and museums and to utilise their facilities as a nucleus for community centres of art and culture. The Federation has already expressed concern at the interpretation of the Government's White Paper "A Policy for the Arts" which has led some local authorities to plan separate accommodation for housing the arts which duplicate the existing provision in the local museum and/or gallery.

STUART M. K. HENDERSON
President.

JOHN BARWICK
Hon. Secretary.

Memorandum by the
Standing Commission on Museums and Galleries

1. The Standing Commission on Museums and Galleries was appointed by Treasury Minute dated 28th November, 1930, on the recommendation of the Royal Commission on Museums and Galleries in their Final Report, Part I, dated 20th September, 1929,

    (i) to advise generally on questions relevant to the most effective development of the National Institutions as a whole, and on any specific questions which may be referred to them from time to time;

    (ii) to promote co-operation between the National Institutions themselves and between the National and Provincial Institutions;

    (iii) to stimulate the generosity and direct the efforts of those who aspire to become public benefactors.

2. More recently the second of its terms of reference has been extended to include advice on the allocation of the Exchequer grants to Area Museum Councils, which were first made available as a result of recommendations in the Standing Commission's Survey of Provincial Museums and Galleries, 1963, in the financial year 1963/64.

3. The Commission has been composed, since 1958, of twelve members of whom one is Chairman, the Chairman and five members being appointed direct by the First Lord of the Treasury and the remaining six members, each of whom represents one of six groups of the National Institutions, by the First Lord on the nomination of the National Institutions.

4. The Commission reported originally to the Chancellor of the Exchequer and since 1965 to the Secretaries of State for Education and Science, Scotland and Wales.

5. The Standing Commission has recently seen the evidence submitted to your Commission by the Scottish Federation of Museums and Art Galleries and I am writing to you on behalf of my colleagues to endorse the recommendations contained in paragraph 8 of this evidence.

6. My colleagues and I would be quite willing to wait upon the Royal Commission to give verbal evidence if this is desired.

Memorandum by the
Institute of Purchasing and Supply

OBJECT: To urge the importance of organising the Supplies Function in the revised structure of local government in Scotland in such a way as to ensure that rate-borne and tax-borne expenditure on the purchase of goods and materials shall secure the benefits which are obtained by the largest industrial and commercial enterprises.

1. The burden of much of the criticism directed at local government has been its failures, real or imagined, to secure maximum benefit for money spent. The Supplies field is essentially one in which local government has to operate within the world of commerce and the manner in which these operations are conducted has become increasingly significant, not only to local government itself, but to the commercial world of which it is so important a customer.

(*Report of the Committee on the Standardisation and Simplification of the Requirements of Local Authorities* (*1934*)
"It is scarcely recognised by the public, and we are not sure that local authorities themselves have fully recognised, how large is the market which they influence. With the ever-expanding duties and assets of local authorities it is open to them, acting on parallel lines (which does not necessarily mean acting in concert or in combination) to exercise a steady influence upon the demand for goods".)

2. The proposals contained in this memorandum are based on the firm conviction that no reorganisation or regrouping of local government units would be complete without statutory powers designed to equip the local government service to undertake its commercial tasks in a commercial way. If the purpose of local government reform is to increase the efficiency of the service, there are few changes in the structure which would result in greater public benefit in terms of increased efficiency and economic advantage.

3. Apart from the economic advantages to be derived, the need for divorcing the functions of purchasing and consuming must always be a vital element of public accountability in the public services. The principle that "the officer in charge of stores should not be the executive officer who is responsible for their consumption" was recommended by the Departmental Committee on Accounts of Local Authorities as long ago as 1907, and this must be regarded as fundamental in any consideration of the future structure of local government.

(*Extract from "Central Purchasing by Local and Public Authorities" 1959, published by The Institute of Municipal Treasurers and Accountants*
"Control of central purchasing arrangements: The unification of purchasing procedures which is necessary to secure many of the aims of central purchasing also renders necessary a unification of the administrative procedures by which purchasing is controlled. . . . Effective control of central purchasing may involve the power of the controlling authority to override the wishes of a user committee or its senior officer. . . . In these circumstances it is important that the controlling authority should be independent of all user committees and that its powers should be clearly defined and understood. For these reasons we feel that a central purchasing committee should be established to which the powers of control over central purchasing arrangements should be delegated.")

4. Buying is a specialist function. This is recognised in industry and commerce, by the Government in relation to the departments which it administers, by public enterprises and the nationalised undertakings, and by the Services. In local government a significant

part of the rate-borne expenditure is involved in the purchase of capital and consumer goods and equipment of all kinds. It is accepted as axiomatic that all other specialist functions, affecting the law, accountancy, architecture, health, civil engineering and other such functions, shall be the responsibility of specialist officers, exclusively concerned with these matters. It is surely no less vital that the purchasing function involved in the acquisition of all the goods and services required by these specialist services should be the responsibility of a specialist buying officer.

(*Extract from "Central Purchasing by Local and Public Authorities" 1959* (see above)
"Staffing: While the need for staff of the highest quality and integrity in all branches of the authority's activities needs no emphasis, in few fields in this need greater than in the field of purchasing.")

(*Extract from the Annual Report of the Supplies Committee of Kent County Council (1964)*)

"As an essential part of this system specialist staff are employed whose duties are concerned not only with the acquisition of goods and the provision of services but with the preparation of specifications, giving assistance to departments in the creation and maintenance of standards of quality and design, standardisation wherever practicable of commodities in general use, and generally ensuring that goods purchased are the most suitable kind for their respective purpose.")

5. The administration of the Supplies function in the public service is concerned with all or any of the processes of purchasing, contracting, provisioning, storing, handling and distributing goods and equipment required by consumer departments for discharging their respective duties. Within local government, Supplies work can also include quality control, costing and accounting, design and technical activities concerned with the preparation of specifications, disposal of all surplus and redundant goods and materials, facilities for the repair and maintenance of a wide range of equipment, and production units for printing, stationery, bookbinding, furniture, etc. In local government a specialised Supplies system almost always includes the management and operation of central stores, although this has not been so generally accepted in Scotland as in England.

6. In Britain as a whole, while most of the larger County Councils and a number of the County Boroughs in England and Wales have recognised the importance of and the advantages to be secured by the operation of a central purchasing organisation, a large number of local authorities have been unwilling or unable to organise the purchasing function in a comparable manner. It is a matter of some surprise, for example, that none of the four large cities in Scotland, representing more than one-third of the total population, has a unified Supplies organisation. The Supplies function is working well in certain County Councils in central Scotland and in these cases there appears to be no doubt about its advantages.

Many existing local government units are, of course, too small to employ specialist officers to run a Supplies department. Regionalisation would provide the perfect framework for efficient functioning of adequately staffed Supplies units.

(*Extract from the Annual Report of the Supplies Committee of Kent County Council, 1964.*)

"Whatever purchasing system is adopted, the administrative work entailed in supplying the needs of . . . establishments is considerable. The necessity for finding suitable sources of supply, obtaining prices, arranging contracts, placing orders, checking the receipt and quality of goods supplied, passing accounts and satisfying the District Auditor that this work has been properly undertaken are inescapable functions for any local authority. If this work is done by individual departments it fails to take advantage of the County Council's considerable purchasing power, and the cost is to a large extent hidden since it is normally difficult, if not impossible, to segregate the cost of the supply function from the other administrative duties of the departments concerned.")

7. The extent to which local government is required to co-ordinate and rationalise its requirements can be an economic factor of importance not only to local authorities but also to industry and commerce. Both in the private and public sectors rationalisation derives largely from the economic advantages to be secured by concentrating purchasing power and by wielding this power from the centre to the advantage of all units within an organisation.

(*Extract from the Second Report of the Committee on the Standardisation and Simplification of the Requirements of Local Authorities (1935)*

"Conclusions:—

(i) that bulk purchase, if it is accompanied by standardisation and simplification, enables better goods to be bought for less money;

(ii) that bulk purchase cannot be operated with maximum success unless the requirements of the buying unit are large enough (*a*) to command large-scale buyers' terms, and (*b*) to employ experienced staff.")

8. It is indicative of the importance now being attached to the Supplies function in local government that, of the reports published by the Local Government Operational Research Unit of the Royal Institute of Public Administration, roughly half have been concerned with aspects of this subject, and the same applies to the research currently being undertaken.

9. The Institute of Purchasing and Supply submits that statutory powers should be provided which:

(*a*) require that each first tier and/or all-purpose authority which may be created, arising out of the reconstruction of local government in Scotland, should appoint a committee to discharge the responsibilities associated with the purchasing function, and should create a separate specialist Supplies department operating under the direction of a specialist Supplies Officer;

(*b*) enable a local authority to purchase and store, and supply to any other local authority in the United Kingdom, any goods and materials required for the discharge of the functions of those authorities;

(*c*) enable a first tier or all-purpose authority to purchase and supply to

(i) any statutory undertaking, any body of persons or any voluntary organisation discharging functions within the area of any first tier or all-purpose authority, and which receives financial aid or contributions from such local authority towards the discharge of its functions;

(ii) any person or body of persons responsible for the management or governing of any school or educational institution in respect of which fees or expenses for any person receiving education or training are wholly or partly defrayed by a local education authority;

(iii) any university or college of education operating wholly or partly within the area of a first tier or all-purpose authority, any goods or materials required for the discharge of the functions of that undertaking.

10. If the proposals contained in this memorandum are accepted as being relevant to the effective and efficient administration of a future local government service, it would seem that statutory powers requiring or enabling authorities to discharge the Supply function in the manner recommended would be essential. Experience shows that resistance to the principle of the separation of the purchasing and the consuming functions can be expected. Resistance from outwith the local government structure itself can and does occur both nationally and locally. From within the local government structure there is inevitably opposition to any proposal to remove the purchasing activity from the control of the consuming service or department who are reluctant to recognise either that purchasing is a specialist function or that a principle of public accountability is involved.

October, 1967.

Printed in Scotland by Her Majesty's Stationery Office Press, Edinburgh
Dd. 227952 K5 8/68 (5304)